JOIN THE
7 FIGURE CLUB

Build Your Business,
Double Profits &
Get Your Life Back

JOIN THE 7 FIGURE CLUB

Build Your Business, Double Profits & Get Your Life Back

Mark Anthony

AAA Training For Success
Long Beach, New York

© 2023 Mark Anthony
All rights reserved.

No part of this publication may be reproduced or transmitted in any form or by any means, mechanical or electronic, including photocopying and recording, or by any information storage and retrieval systems, without permission in writing from the author or publisher (except by a reviewer, who may quote brief passages in a review).

Disclaimer: The advice and strategies contained in this book may not be suitable for every situation. This work is sold with the understanding that the Author and Publisher are not engaged in rendering legal, accounting or other professional services. Neither the Author nor the Publisher shall be liable for damages arising herefrom. The fact that an organization or website is referred to in this book as a citation or a potential source of further information does not mean that the Author or Publisher endorses the information that the organization or website may provide or recommendations those may make. Further, readers should be aware that websites listed in this work may have been changed or disappeared between when this work was written and when it is read.

Published by AAA Training For Success, Long Beach, New York

Paperback ISBN 979-8-9881353-2-6
Kindle ISBN979-8-9881353-1-9
Library of Congress Control Number: 2023907334

Website address: https://JoinThe7FigureClub.com

FIRST EDITION

Cover Design: Danijela Mijailovic
Editing: Evan Slawson
Interior Book Design: Danijela Mijailovic

This book is dedicated to my mother and father, who inspired my entrepreneurial spirit and instilled the work ethic to make it happen.

GET FREE

Join The 7 Figure Club

Bonus Material & Resources

Register on JoinThe7FigureClub.com

TABLE OF CONTENTS

Introduction: The 7 Figure Club Formula	1
Pillar 1: Mindset — *Own* Don't *Operate*	7
Pillar 2: Accountability — Commitment to Goals	35
Pillar 3: Sales — Get More Faster	61
Pillar 4: Marketing — Scaling Your Sales	105
Pillar 5: Customer Service — The Secret Sauce	163
Pillar 6: Negotiation — Becoming a Master	185
Pillar 7: Processes — Getting Your Life Back	207
Get Your Free 7 Figure Club Resources	231

Introduction
THE 7 FIGURE CLUB FORMULA

Starting a business is one of the hardest and most courageous things you have ever done. It required you to choose a path many speak of, but few actually set out on. It required you to take bold action. It required you to break out of your comfort zone.

As you know, starting the business was only the first step. Then you had to grow sales and prove you had a viable business that generates a significant income, which is a totally different game with a new set of challenges.

This book is designed specifically for you. It is a step-by-step roadmap that shows six-figure business owners how to become 7-figure business owners by overcoming growing pains and eliminating the landmines that block sales and hinder profitability.

In order to build a highly profitable seven-figure business and become a member of the 7 Figure Club, you must learn to understand how your mindset and your beliefs serve you -- and also sabotage you.

Mindset is the foundation upon which you will build 7 figure business habits. Mindset is your determination to achieve the goals you have set. Belief is the force that keeps you going.

You will establish easy-to-implement methods to rapidly grow and sustain sales. You will learn how to match marketing tools to your business rather than getting hooked into the latest marketing fad. The only marketing you need is one that gives you a positive return on your marketing spend. Most important of all, you will learn the required business processes that get you out of working in your business. The goal is to be a highly profitable business *owner*, NOT to be an overworked founder of a business.

Like you, I've always been an entrepreneur. Even as a kid, I always found a way to hustle and make some money working for myself. In my twenties, I started my first real business, grew it into the six figures, and made some good money. In my forties, I built a profitable 7-figure business and in my fifties, I developed a substantial 8-figure business exceeding over $100 million in sales. Best of all, it required the fewest amount of my hours. I truly owned a business, rather than the business owning me. I'm not going to say it was easy, but it was not nearly as hard as you might think.

Once you know the formula it gets even easier. It's interesting how one person can have multiple successful businesses, and other people struggle to have just one. Successful entrepreneurs duplicate their successes. If you took away their business and their resources, they would each be able to build it back quickly. Members of the 7 Figure Club follow a formula that repeatedly grows both sales and profits. Best of all, it also allows them to have more time to enjoy the things that matter most.

Each chapter of this book gives you the required pieces of the 7 Figure Club formula, and how to use it to grow your business, make it more profitable, do so quickly, and do it in a way that is duplicable, if you so choose.

It's my story and that of the many 7 and 8 figure business owners I've had the privilege to work with and help. It is our pleasure to help other entrepreneurs quickly and profitably grow their business too. Our lessons learned the hard way will be shared here to make it easier for you to take your business to the next level.

I call these chapters "Pillars" because each one focuses on an aspect of building your business to the 7-figure level. I call them Pillars rather than Steps because they don't have to be done in any particular order. But they all have to be done.

Each Pillar stands on its own and supports the small business. Combined together they leverage one another to create the foundation for becoming the one out of ten small businesses that do over one million in sales.

Putting your income in the top 1% by building a business that is larger and more profitable than 90% of businesses is achievable and realistic when you utilize each of the pillars of our 7 Figure Club formula.

Here's what's in store for you in the pages that follow:

Pillar 1: Mindset — *Own* Don't *Operate*

The typical self-employed business operator is overworked and underpaid. If that's you, that is about to change. Your new mindset, goals and structured plan will be the foundation for your growth, profitability, and freedom.

Pillar 2: Accountability — Commitment to Goals

The accountability dashboard will give you the structure to build an organization. Most importantly, you will learn to hold everyone *accountable* to following the plan, achieving results, and doing so without wasting the most precious resource of all, time.

Pillar 3: Sales — Get More Faster

Sales will help you build cash flow. Cash flow is the resource that sustains your growth. Cash flow comes from *sales*. Every businessperson must be able to sell and use that ability to set the business up for a steady flow of sales.

Pillar 4: Marketing — Scaling Your Sales

Marketing is the process of creating sales opportunities. It takes many forms. Understanding your options and selecting the right marketing will allow you to fuel 7 Figure Club sales growth.

Pillar 5: Customer Service — The Secret Sauce

Good customer service results in repeat orders, returning customers and increasing your average order size. This is what will exponentially grow your business. Repeat business is your most profitable sale. It only happens when you have happy customers. Happy customers come from a company culture of An Award Winning level of service.

Pillar 6: Negotiation — Becoming a Master

As you grow the stakes get bigger and bigger. Your ability to negotiate larger transactions, higher stake contracts, and much more is essential. Negotiate the right deals and you will win the big opportunities.

Pillar 7: Processes — Getting Your Life Back

Make the business work for you (not the other way around).

Your ability to create *processes* allows you to have a business that works for you. It becomes a vehicle that can give you a substantial income and a great lifestyle without being chained to a job.

PILLAR 1
MINDSET — *OWN* DON'T *OPERATE*

Mindset is very possibly the biggest difference between struggling entrepreneurs and those that have scaled their business to seven and eight figures.

The first essential building block of mindset is to recognize you must be a business *owner* rather than someone who is self-employed and runs a business.

To have the business you own provide the lifestyle you desire, properly structured goals are essential. When you become a high goal achiever rather than a "someday I will" dreamer, and guide those around you to do the same, you are on the path to being an influential leader who has the foundation in place to create a highly profitable seven figures business.

Realizing Your 7 Figure Potential

Becoming an entrepreneur is exciting. The journey is exhilarating. It is full of possibility. You have brought a passion project to life, turned a dream into reality, and so much more. Of course it's a bit scary, but that fear is no match for the strength and confidence pulsing through your veins. Every business owner remembers that moment they conceived the concept for their business, the day it launched, and each of the early days of nurturing their idea into a real business. The good times, the scary times, the hard times, the sacrifices, and everything it took to create a rewarding sustainable business.

Congratulations, you made it through the business's infancy and the toddler stage. Your baby has now grown to the level of a sustainable business that is somewhere in the six-figure range. As your business grows, the demands and challenges change. You have solved numerous problems and your business is now a somewhat independent but highly needy teenager. You've traded one set of issues for a new set of issues, often with more zeros behind the dollar sign associated with them. One day your business is solid and strong, and then the next, in desperate need of your attention.

Your goal is to get the business you raised out of the turbulent needy stages and grow it to that of an independent and wildly successful business. To graduate your business into the ranks of the prestigious 7 Figure Club, or even the Elite 8 Figure category, requires you to transition from being a hands-on operator to an owner who scales with systems.

You have the heart, you have the desire, and by your following our 7 Figure Club process and best practices we will give you, the specific frameworks needed to grow profitably. In addition, you will gain the time and freedom every business should give its owner. We will cover each of the core elements of building that seven-figure business, and the steps required to execute each effectively. You will have a simplified process that will allow you to achieve what fewer than 1 in 10 business owners are able to accomplish.

They fall short not due to lack of desire, effort, skill or passion. Instead they fall short of breaking through the ceilings of $1,000,000 in sales and then $10,000,000 in sales because they fail to unify each of the key business components into one tightly executed process.

Be an Owner Not an Operator

Like you, I remember the day I started my first real business. It was a sports publishing company. We produced game programs for college sporting events in the New York City area. In only a few short years, I had developed licensing agreements with colleges and universities all across the country. I could drive across the country and in almost every state, there was at least one school we represented. There were only a few gaps in the country where I did not work with a school. Funny thing is, I was so young and inexperienced I didn't even know what a licensing agreement was at the time. It is amazing how far drive and determination can take you.

The journey started at the age of 19. I worked my butt off for a guy selling ads for a firm that produced game-day programs. UCONN football was the first account I worked on. I took the training seriously, and the commission I was earning even more so. Each day I made a sale, I was so proud. At dinner, I boasted to mom and dad about all the calls I made, how my presentations went and of course which prospects I closed.

The new kid in the office was quickly closing more new sales than anyone else in the office. Others made more sales, representing accounts with much higher ad rates, and a much larger base of repeat customers. But I was willing to prospect, call, and present. The end result was more *new* ad accounts were opened than anyone else.

How was I rewarded? With broken promises. Based on the numbers and the agreement made with my employer, I had earned a commission of about $625 after my draw on commission. A lot of money to a 19-year-old kid in college especially back then. Easily several thousand today.

But I never saw the money. I was given a variety of excuses why I couldn't be paid and I accepted each of them, for a while. Finally it became clear that this was not the case of a business cycle needing to be completed in terms of billing and collection, and instead an example of someone just putting off paying a "kid." Another example of an employer looking out for themselves and not taking care of the people working hard to make it happen.

Damn, that pissed me off. So what's a boy to do? Yup, I took him to court and won. Better than that, I knew of several local colleges in the NYC area that were looking for someone to represent their school and take on the task of advertising. Schools that had also considered my former employer as a viable vendor.

Knock, knock. I went and met with two schools, one of which was the prestigious Columbia University, and they both gave me the nod. I had my first two clients. I headed downtown, registered my business and then opened my first business bank account with $100, which was all my savings. I didn't ask parents, friends, or family for a dime.

I knew a little about selling ads, very little about laying out a sports magazine, zero about invoicing, or how to run a business. I did know how to *work*. I did know how to lean into things and apply myself. What I did not know I could learn.

Within seven years I had schools all across the country and a profitable little six-figure business. I was on my way. Sweetest part of all, I had an office outside my home, 15 Park Row, in lower Manhattan near Wall Street. It gets even sweeter. That was the office of the firm that didn't pay me my commission. I had taken over their business.

We each have a story that puts us on our entrepreneurial quest. Each of us will have some really big obstacles to overcome. Each one of us has the ability to do so. Each one of us has the opportunity to turn their business into one that is a member of the 7 Figure Club. You can then build on those successes and become part of the "Elite 8," a business doing eight figures, or over $10,000,000 per year in sales. Turn your challenges into opportunities. It may not seem that way at the time but recognizing your greatest growth really does come when you are challenged.

The 7 Figure Mindset

The journey is fantastic. It starts with that mindset shift where you chose to stop working for someone else, to take the leap, and start your own enterprise. You may not have realized it at first, but you chose to define yourself differently. You decided to no longer be someone who would work for someone else.

A truly special moment.

To grow to 7 figures quickly, you need to make another mindset shift. The faster you make this shift, the faster your business will grow and the more profitable your business will be. And most important, the faster you make the shift, the more rapidly you will gain the freedom and time you desire from owning your own business.

It took me years to recognize this. I selected the wrong mindset out of the gate. I maintained the wrong mindset for years. The mistake I made is that when I started my own business, I became SELF-EMPLOYED.

SELF-EMPLOYED is where you trade the 40-hour workweek for the 80-hour workweek, plus take on additional responsibilities and far more risk. When we choose to start a business we are willing to take the risk of long hours for possibly fewer dollars. We choose this for the potential of a reward, knowing we'll be paid less in the beginning. *Maybe even being paid less forever.*

That is madness, and we are going to change that. We are going to break the cycle.

It is a risk we are willing to take. It is in our DNA to go for it. We are risk takers. We are reward seekers. We are the people who go for it, rather than living our lives saying, "if only" or "what if."

Taking on the quest to have a highly profitable 7 figure or even an 8 figure plus business, is the game we choose to take on. At times it's tough, at times it is even brutal, but we revel in our victory.

We are "Business Gladiators."

More importantly, we are "*VICTORIOUS* Business Gladiators."

Change How You Define Yourself

If you identify yourself as self-employed, please change that immediately! Stop defining yourself as "self-employed." ELIMINATE the term "self-employed" as it refers to you.

YOU ARE A BUSINESS OWNER. PERIOD.

What's the difference? Someone who is self-employed has a business they work in. They, by definition, have created their own *job*. They show up to work in that business. They have a specific role, probably multiple roles, that requires their presence, expertise and attention. They are operating the business.

Someone that is self-employed is a *business operator*, a person who works in the daily operations of the business.

PILLAR 1: Mindset

Your new MINDSET from this moment forward is that you are a *business owner.*

Business owners, on the other hand, *oversee* their businesses. The business pays the owner, and the business owner *manages* rather than *operates*. The business owner spends time in the business by choice. The business owner can choose to structure the business where they are not even there, yet they are still paid handsomely from the business they created.

The goal is to HAVE A BUSINESS ON YOUR TERMS.

Structure it to look the way you want.

Structure it to give you the lifestyle that is right for you.

The faster you make this mindset shift, the faster you will get there.

For well over two decades, I referred to myself as self-employed. I was proud to tell people I was a self-employed business owner. It became part of my identity. But I was wrong. It trapped me into being my own employee. For years I did not recognize this. Because of that I operated within the business. I made choices, and decisions as an "operator" rather than as an owner. Learn from my mistake.

In the early years of the business you will likely need to spend more time in multiple facets of the business. Yes, expect the hours to be long. But, like each and every goal, when you know clearly where you are going, you make decisions that get you there in a much faster straight line. When you know *why* you are doing something and the specific outcomes you are looking to achieve, you structure your actions accordingly. Clarity is power.

Change how you see yourself early on in the journey. Many business owners refer to the business as their "baby." It is one of their "children" so to speak. They created it. You would not raise your children to be dependent on you forever. In the early years, you know dependence on you will be higher, but all along your goal is to raise that child to be self-sufficient, highly independent and a thriving individual who is highly successful on their own.

A parent who achieves that is successful. That is their role.

Do the same thing for your business.

Raise it to be highly independent. You can choose your level of involvement, but raise your business to thrive without you.

Climb Mountains

My dear friend Jenn has a highly successful financial software firm. She is a powerful and dynamic woman and her business is successful by any and every definition. She built the business, put time into the business, and was proud of the business.

On a Tuesday afternoon around 4 p.m., she was in a devastating car crash. She was broadsided, and her car was totaled. Jaws of Life were required to pull her from the wreckage. Thankfully, miraculously, she was able to walk away without even a scratch.

It was a life-defining moment that made her see that everything could truly change in an instant. In that instant, she assessed where she wanted to be, who she wanted to be with and where she wanted to be spending her time.

Where she wanted to spend her time wasn't in the business. It was with her family, and it was taking on new challenges including educating people via a podcast (*Take A Break With Jenn Drummond*) and inspiring women to achieve their full potential. Her message was about defying limitations.

PILLAR 1: Mindset

Once she recognized this, she "hired herself out of a job," as she puts it, She hired her own replacement so she could be free to achieve her new goals.

She achieved each, while also being a single mom of seven. Being a business owner, rather than a business operator gave her the freedom and the resources to truly pursue and attain her dreams.

Jenn became the first woman to summit each of the second-highest peaks worldwide, including being only the third woman to conquer K2, the world's deadliest mountain.

Own a business that gives you the life you desire not the job you want.

The 70% Rule — Developing Your Team

A big part of becoming the owner, and removing yourself from being an operator, is developing your team. The faster you release yourself from the significance — meaning "ego gratification" — that comes from being the expert, the master, or the "genius" that comes from doing a given task better than anyone else, the faster you will enter the 7 Figure Club.

In each of my businesses, I was fortunate to recognize this lesson, and put the principle into play. In my publishing business, I cloned myself by developing my sales team. I recognized that if *I* called on 10 qualified prospects I would close 90% of them. That was a darn good close rate. Despite some excellent training, the best I could get my sales team to was a 70% close rate.

However, I also realized that realistically I could meet with maybe 10 people a week. That meant the maximum number of sales I could make was 10, and that was an unrealistic expectation. When I was in the zone, 9 was about as good as it would ever get. As I hired and trained reps I found that 8 reps closing 70% of the prospects led to far more sales than I could even come close to on my own. Those 8 reps were bringing in over 50 sales in a week. Yes, a few prospects were not closed that I might have been able to close but my team reached far more prospects than I ever could and therefore closed more sales than I ever could.

One day the phone rang and I picked up. It was a sales lead, and I realized it had been so long since I made a presentation that I said, "Hold on let me put you through to Michael." In that moment, I realized the training and processes we implemented had developed a staff in the sales department that surpassed my abilities. I was thrilled.

Get yourself out of each department as you grow your business.

> **Side note:** Michael's skills continued to develop, and when it was time for us to part ways he got a job with one of the leading print advertising firms in the nation and he grew to become one of their sales managers. Develop your people, and truly be committed to helping them reach their highest potential.

The same thing happened multiple times with the digital agency I created. As the face of the business, the owner and the person that brought in many of the clients, it was natural that clients wanted to speak to me when questions would arise. The client's questions could have been strategy related, ranking related, or something tied to a paid ad budget. In each case, my goal was to develop the team's skills, and have the business grow to a level where Jordan, Pedrito or another member of the team, could answer the questions even better than I could.

PILLAR 1: Mindset

Make yourself obsolete in your own business. Make your business grow to be independent of you. This gives you freedom. This gives you scalability. This increases your profits. This increases the ability to sell your business if you decide you want an exit plan. This has you living the life of a business owner and no longer being stuck in the role of business operator.

Congratulations, you are on the road to raising a great business.

In the book *Think and Grow Rich* by Napoleon Hill there is a story about Henry Ford being brought into court where was challenged on not knowing how to do many things. He was called ignorant. He was confronted about all his shortcomings. His reply was that he didn't need to know the answers. His genius was in having assembled a team where he could press any one of 50 buttons and an expert member of his staff would come running to his office with the answer that was needed.

For over 100 years the formula has remained the same: Build a team that sets you free to do what you do best. Build a business that allows you to choose your level of involvement.

The formula was true for Henry Ford, Jenn, me and countless other business people that have scaled their business, and it all starts with the mindset of being the OWNER, Not the operator.

> **PRO TIP:** Eliminate the term "self-employed" business owner from your vocabulary and mindset. You are a business owner.

You must be — and think of yourself as — the *owner*, rather than a self-employed business *operator*. Remember that you are not looking for a job, you are looking for the financial freedom and personal time/independence a thriving business gives you. Without an owner mindset it is nearly impossible to scale your business to where it provides the freedom of time and resources you desire.

Own, DON'T *operate*!

Set Measurable Goals

Most business owners have big dreams but they are undermined by weak goals. You must have both: big dreams and big goals.

Dreams are great. Goals are better. Much better. When you redefine your dreams, and restate them in the form of strong goals you have taken an idea, a wish, a strong desire, and turned it into a something solid, and tangible.

To turn your dreams into goals you MUST put them in writing.

In addition to putting them in writing, you must follow a specific formula. If you skip the formula you will slow the pace at which you achieve your goals.

Building a 7 Figure Club business is based on achieving many goals. The fastest way to achieve those goals is to make sure they are properly planned and stated.

The STAR M Formula

More money is a universal goal. When you ask people about their top 3 goals, "more money" is almost always mentioned. The formula to make that happen is something I call the STAR M formula.

STAR M stands for Specific goals, Time frame, Achievable, Realistic and Measurable.

For instance, someone says their goal for this year is to have more money. Here's how the STAR M formula can help them turn their wish into a solid goal:

Step 1: Be specific

In workshops, when I ask people about their goals someone always shouts out "more money." I reach into my pocket and happily give them a dollar or two. I congratulate them on achieving their "goal." I asked them how they feel having so quickly achieved their goal, and so easily, just by shouting out more money. And yes they are saying, "Hold on, that's not what I meant." They point out that they wanted much more than two dollars. I'm happy to help, so I hand them a five. I let them know they got 150% more instantly, surely they must be happy now. I smile, and playfully state, "Well done, you achieved your goal."

Obviously, a couple of dollars is not what they wanted. But how much did they want? I don't know, you don't know, and based on what they said, *they* don't know.

The first step is to clearly state what you want. You must be specific. Specific in a way that everyone would be able to understand what the goal is. Is it $100 more? Is it $100,000 more? Maybe it is $500,000 more, or a $1,000,000. Each of us understands the specifics in those examples. What's most important is that you are so specific that you have a clear picture of the goal. It is crystal clear in your mind's eye. You see it, you picture it. You recognize it. That all comes from being SPECIFIC.

Step 2: The Time Frame

Let's say your goal was to make $250,000 more in income. The goal was achieved, but it took 5 years to make it happen. Are you happy? For one person the answer might be yes. For someone else that time frame would be totally unacceptable. You must have a specific date in mind. You need to have a defined time target.

Without the target, the precious resource of time wastes away. Your specific time frame will be essential in fueling urgency and tracking progress.

Step 3: Achievable

I really believe that *anything we clearly and specifically envision in our mind's eye is achievable.*

Once you clearly see the vision, all you have to do is consistently take focused action towards it and you will achieve what you desire.

Step 4: Realistic

This is a tricky one and often seems to be at odds with step 3. Many goals that are specific for a particular time frame are very achievable. However, based on other variables it might not be realistic. Let's stick with our example where you want to increase your income by $250,000 per year and you want this to happen in one year.

This is absolutely achievable for a high percentage of business owners.

$250K IS TOTALLY DOABLE. But is it realistic based on *your* situation and what you are willing to do to make it happen?

In all my years of coaching and training everyone says it is "totally doable." They tell me how they will do whatever it takes. When it comes to implementing the, "whatever it takes" actions, they start to list numerous reasons, responsibilities, challenges or justifications as to why they are not getting things done. They explain why they are off pace. They explain why their numbers are low. Who cares about their excuses? If they want to achieve their goal they must solve the problems, or recognize that some adjustment might be needed. Often only the time frame needs to be tweaked. Hitting $250K in profit is specific and achievable, BUT it might not be realistic to do it in 6 months based on where they are in their business journey or the resources they are working with.

If you can only work part time, making the $250K in 6 months might not be realistic. If your capacity is limited to 5 additional clients, it might not be realistic. If you need more production capacity — and that is going to take 6 months to put in place — that could potentially make achieving the specific goal unrealistic in a particular time frame.

"Realistic" and "achievable" are ways to create a checks-and-balance system which is an excellent way to access your very achievable goal. A checks-and-balance system is an essential step to help map out your timeline. It helps define what resources you will commit to in order to make your big goal happen. It will also help you define what you will give up while pursuing your big goal.

If you are going to put an extra 15 hours a week into an aspect of your business (sales, marketing, team development, process creation, etc.) that 15 hours has to come from someplace else. Be realistic about what you are willing to trade, as well as what you are truly willing to implement.

Step 5: Measurable

The "M" of STAR M stands for Measurable. I often like to think it stands for Mark, but it really stands for Measurable. You need to be able to clearly track your progress. To do this, you must be able to measure the actions that are contributing to your progress and track your results in terms of where they are at any point along the way, compared to what was projected.

If you want $250K in additional income your progress should be continually measured. It might be daily, weekly or monthly. You must monitor the journey. This must be done *in writing*.

You must be able to clearly measure if you are on pace, off pace or ahead of schedule. For example, you may need to measure the number of meetings with potential customers, the number of proposals presented, as well as revenues brought in.

To make your dreams and ideas transform into achievable goals, the goals must be in writing. It is not a goal unless it is written.

> **PRO TIP:** When your staff creates goals for their roles, or their departments make sure they also follow the STAR M formula. That will literally assure you are all on the same page as you read what they wrote and see how they defined the goal.

When you utilize ALL of the steps in the STAR M formula, and it is ALL documented IN WRITING, you have the foundation for a goal achievement plan.

Using STAR M for Goals Beyond Business

The STAR M Formula is applicable to goal-setting in each and every area of your life. As a 7 Figure Club business owner, you expect to have both the money and time to live richly in every aspect of your life. To make that happen, create clear written goals for each area of your life where you want to create the biggest leaps. It is also a great gift for your children to teach them how to apply the STAR M formula long before they are pursuing finance goals. The more you apply goal achievement to multiple categories of your life the more you will master the formula.

The more you guide family, friends and team members to pursue goals, rather than talk about dreams, the more you will become a powerful influencer in their life. Teaching others how to properly set a goal is a wonderful gift to give those you care about. It will improve their lives tremendously. Their ability to set goals will transition them from a "Someday I Will Dreamer" into a "High Goal Achiever."

Here are a few examples for writing goals using STAR M in life

Weight Loss

"My goal is to lose 10 pounds in 22 weeks thus attaining my desired weight of ____ by the specific date of ____."

This is achievable and realistic because it only requires losing half a pound per week and gives a 2-week cushion. I know it is realistic because I can easily reduce calorie intake by 250 calories per day and my family has committed to stop eating any cookies, candy or desserts in front of me. They've even agreed not to keep those things in the house. Each Saturday morning, I will weigh myself and chart my progress. I will also write on the calendar where I expect my weight to have dropped down to. This way I'm monitoring short term progress and seeing whether I'm on pace to meet the goal I set for myself.

Education

"I am going to raise my math grade from a C to a B or higher this semester."

This is both realistic and achievable by doing my math homework first while I'm most alert. I've committed to doing it in 25-minute study blocks with no distractions which includes turning my phone off during each 25-minute study block. I also have the support of the math teacher — and a free tutor if needed. Lastly, mom and dad said I can skip doing the dishes if I'm immediately studying right after dinner with no phone, TV or other distractions. My progress is easily judged by measuring my class participation, tracking test results, and monitoring progress with my teacher during the semester rather than waiting till midterms and final exam results.

Passing Real Estate License Exam

"I will pass the real estate test in 12 weeks."

I will enroll in the real estate course that starts on September 17 and attend class two evenings per week for the next 12 weeks. I will also block out 30 minutes on Saturday and Sunday mornings for additional study.

This is both achievable and realistic since I will drive to the course right from work twice a week. I know that the real estate license will help give me additional lifetime income that will improve the quality of my life and that of my family. Studying for a half-hour twice on the weekend can easily be scheduled by eliminating some TV watching. If I really want to watch a given show I will choose to record it, and watch it after I'm done with my 30-minute study block. My progress is easily measured by keeping pace with the course curriculum.

Leaders are High Goal Achievers

Leaders focus on high performance and help those around them maximize potential.

As the owner of a 7 Figure Club Business it is your role to define the goals and make sure the business is on pace and on course to achieving it.

Leaders need strong goals to inspire their team, and those goals can be wildly big. Be clear, honest, and REALISTIC about what it is going to take to make it happen. Recognize what must be put in place to make it happen, what resources must be committed, and how actions and results will be measured.

Define Wealthy

One of the Big Reasons you probably want to have a 7 Figure Club business is to be "wealthy." An important aspect of that is to actually define "wealthy." It shows up in many ways, among them are "time" and "money."

We all want more time and more money. Both are important resources. We can always make more money but we can't make more time, so time is an especially precious resource. Therefore, we must be more aware of how we allocate it. That awareness can transform your business and your life.

Know where you are and where you want to go

Time is a challenge for everyone. At every stage of life you still only have 7 days and 24 hours to work with. Recognize that if you are 45 and have a 10-year-old playing Pop Warner football, you only have a handful of seasons to watch them play. Maybe 30 games? Skip a bunch and you never get them back. Entrepreneur and author Jesse Itzler mentioned how he loved to ski with his kids but they realistically could only do one ski vacation a year because of scheduling issues. Based on his age, he might only have ten more ski seasons left.

Thinking about it like that hit me powerfully, and I'm so happy to give you that reminder, too.

If you only have 10 or 20 opportunities to do something the way you really want to do it, each time you skip an opportunity it is a significant percentage of the opportunities available to you, and you'll never got those lost opportunities back.

If you have ten ski seasons ahead of you and you put off three of them, 30 percent of that opportunity is gone.

If there are twenty home games in four years of high school, and you're too busy to make any games one season, then you've lost 25% of your chances to see your kid play.

We don't know how much time we have, but the clock is ticking. Remember the time to start getting your life back is now, and that starts with building a business you own rather than one you operate.

Planning to make each year your best year ever

This past year I've skied Aspen, Park City, and Vail, climbed Mount Washington, learned to fly fish, participated in a Top Gun school where you fly a real plane during an aerial dog fight versus your friends (I won!) and journeyed to the Arctic on a polar bear expedition. The highlight was spending a month in Italy fulfilling a bucket-list experience for my 90-year old parents. And these are merely a few of the awesome highlights.

This only happens by planning your year.

One of the ways I like to plan such an amazing year is by spending New Year's Eve staying in. I spend the rest of the year working effectively, going out, and doing meaningful things in each area of my life. The rest of the year is spent growing sales, growing the business, having fun with friends and family all year, traveling more than most, helping various causes, growing spiritually, intellectually, and more. The LAST thing I want to do on New Year's Eve is to go out!

Most people spend more time planning a vacation than on how to achieve their goals. That is the reason I created the ritual of using New Year's Eve to specifically focus on all I achieved in the prior year, and all I want to achieve and attract into my life for the coming year. Rather than starting the year being tired from a late night of over-eating, over-drinking and over-spending, I wake up early on New Year's Day, energized and focused on creating the momentum for another fulfilling year.

I don't mean to sound arrogant, but I do want to make a point. This may sound weird, but I believe most of the things I mentioned above happen BECAUSE I DO NOT GO OUT on New Year's Eve. Instead, I have a different ritual. For the last 25 years I've used New Year's Eve as the time to map out my upcoming year. Plan to make this your best year ever and have every year keep getting better and better. As a friend Jesse Itzler likes to say, "Build your life resume."

It also helps when you have created that powerful "why." A powerful "why" develops clarity on your motivations. Whenever you take on a big goal it requires more than saying "yes" to that goal. It requires you saying "no" to many other things in life. Many of those other things are going to be highly pleasurable, enjoying and rewarding. They will become distractions to your big goal. You will be tempted to justify your tending to those other things.

Although they may also be important, it is that singular focus on your big goal that creates the momentum. The greater your clarity on your "why," and how achieving your goal will improve your life, the more you will stay the course and maintain your focus.

Why do you want to have your own business? Why do you want to be a highly profitable member of the 7 Figure Club? Why do you want your year to look a certain way with specific new outcomes?

Have clear strong motivating answers that drive you to take the actions required to become a member of the 7-Figure Club.

My New Year's Eve Ritual

First, I have my favorite luxurious meal. I like to dine in and make the meal myself. I also open a really nice bottle of wine. Something that is a real treat. After enjoying this amazing feast, it is time to notice the wins and be grateful for them.

Second, I take out a new journal and write down all the wins from the prior year. In each category of life, I list all the things I was really pleased about, and grateful for. I list all the habits and consistent actions I took to make those wins happen. I take note of which ones I want to maintain. Then I list all the things I wanted to do, but didn't take action on or complete. I take inventory of what is required to make progress on those, and assess whether I really want to take action on it.

Third, I do a creative, think big, think fun, think profitable STAR M goal-setting session utilizing the STAR M formula outlined previously. This session is at least 60 minutes, preferably at least two hours, and when really in the zone, several hours. The longer the writing session goes the better. I get greater clarity on what matters most and what I really want to attract in the coming year.

I've found that my goal-setting focus for this ritual is influenced by those I share it with. This is actually a reason why I often like to spend all or part of this evening on my own.

When I'm with people that fully embrace this ritual and are equally charged by the power of choosing to create their best life, the more effective I am at manifesting the New Year's vision. When our mutual priority is on designing an amazing life, we fuel one another's ability to attract what we desire. When you live a life where you are a high performer in every area, it is truly great. When *I'm* going strong *they* are motivated to look deeper, and get more clarity too. When *I* start to run out of steam and see *them* looking at more and more areas it inspires me to do the same.

Certainly the opposite is true too. When I've been with people that write down a few sentences for a few areas of life and they are done in 30 minutes and "patiently" watch me, I've found it limiting. Although they say, "Don't rush" and "Take your time" it creates a pressure that is hard for me to overlook. If you embrace this ritual as I have, share it only with those who fuel you.

If you would like to participate in a complimentary "Quick Start to the New Year" goal-setting experience, register on **www.JoinThe7FigureClub.com** and we will send over the details. It is a deep dive where we go through the process with a group of like-minded people. A fun and empowering way to kick things off.

People will say, "Do it New Year's Day," "Do it one day next week," or some other alternative. They will suggest going to some fabulous event, party, or concert, and it will be tempting. But after decades of doing my goal-setting ritual, I've found many of the activities of my year and the way my year is lived are, for me, way better than their New Year's Eve suggestions. I'd rather design my year, a year filled with success, one that creates the foundation for future years, rather than go out solely because it's New Year's Eve.

I look forward to the start of each new year. I'm ready to embrace all the opportunity it brings, and have a solutions mindset to take on any challenges as each of the New Year's goals is pursued. I've found the best way to accomplish each goal is to create momentum right from day one. That means taking some immediate action on my new goals, even if it is a small action on New Year's Day.

The key is make sure you start the year with a powerful, clear goal-setting session where everything for the year gets mapped out.

I worked with someone who appreciated everything I shared about the importance of the session and carved out the time to do it. They scheduled with me for February 10th. They told me about the special New Year's Eve party and New Year's Day brunch. Their wife's birthday the next week, then a business trip and a few other justifications to keep delaying the session, even though they appreciated the importance of the goal-setting plan.

During our one-on-one coaching session, I pointed out that we were already 10% into the year at week 5. They had already lost 10% of their time to have a year fully focused on proactively steering the ship. Those first 5 weeks had

PRO TIP: *Quarterly reviews are a must.* After your New Year's Eve session, review your goal-setting details and the plan you mapped out every quarter as well. See what is working, and what needs tweaking or course-correcting.

been spent on "important" things that "kept coming up." Once they recognized this, they saw the power of doing it on December 31. They were converted into fellow New Year's Eve goal setters from that moment on. Find the time that's right for you, but make it happen early.

Fourth: I put up a big wall calendar. One where you can see the entire year all at once. Using a variety of colored sticky notes, small ones so they fit on each day in the wall calendar, one per date, I write goals and plans on each and stick them on. I use multiple colors randomly mostly because I like to see a variety of color posted, but you could also use one color for business, another for fun with family, another for travel, etc. There is no right or wrong. The power is in:

a) Slowing down enough to recognize what you want,

b) Blocking out the time for what matters most, including kids, adventures, family trips, business trips, anything that's important for you to make happen during the upcoming year,

c) And seeing at a glance the amazing upcoming year that your highly profitable business will allow you to have.

There is magic in this process: Once the time is blocked out you have taken a major step toward committing to making it happen. You have made each experience desired more real, and that makes your "why" more concrete.

These are all essential steps to getting your life back, and living it on your terms. When other invitations want to encroach on that time, and there will be many, you are physically required to peel off the sticky note. You are taking away the event, the experience you said you wanted. Are you going to transfer it to another part of the year, or are you going to toss that experience in the trash? That is *powerful*. Time is limited, resources are limited, and you must choose wisely.

I've done this ritual for decades, using a notebook or journal and a calendar to write down my goals and plan out my year. When my friend and mentor Jesse Itzler, the founder of Zico Coconut Water and Marquis Jets, shared his own similar approach to this process, it allowed me to visualize everything I wanted even more clearly. I highly recommend you check out his excellent full-year calendar-planning tool at www.BuildYourLifeResume.com

He sells a massive wall calendar that folds up into a file-folder-sized packet along with some additional support tools that are fantastic.

> **PRO TIP:** Each choice impacts other choices. When you say "yes" to one choice it also means saying "no" to several others. Be aware of your choices. Know where your choices are leading you. Recognize where those choices are taking you for both the near and far term. Building the biggest and most profitable business at the expense of your family and well-being is not the game plan. Set your goals, plan your actions, and have clarity about the choices you make in order to live a life where you have it all. Enjoy the journey as well as the destination.

Remember being a business *owner* rather than a business operator will give you both the money and the TIME to create the life you desire. The life you desire makes it worthwhile to put in the effort on each step of growing a highly profitable 7 Figure Club Business.

> **PRO TIP:** Money, combined with the experiences you desire with those you love most is living with abundance. You can have it all. The choice is yours.

In Summary: Everything is Mindset

- Want more sales & higher revenues — Mindset
- Want to be a millionaire — it starts with Mindset
- Want to be a better leader — have a leader Mindset
- Want to be calm in an entrepreneurial storm — Mindset
- Want to achieve each and every goal — it is all about Mindset
- Want to increase sales, increase profits, and get your life back — Mindset

The 7 Figure Club Business Owner has the mindset, but they also have something few entrepreneurs have, and that is 24/7 *accountability*. That is a level of accountability that is unmatched by over 90% of business owners. That accountability comes from their focus and their ability to track progress, as well as the actions that drive that progress.

PILLAR 2
ACCOUNTABILITY —
COMMITMENT TO GOALS

> *What gets measured gets improved.* — Peter Drucker
>
> When a stat is measured it improves. When each department is accountable to posting their results and the specific actions that drive those results, rapid growth occurs. Your commitment to knowing your organization's numbers is proportionate to how fast you achieve 7 Figure Club status.
>
> Knowing *where you were, where you are* and *where you are going* is essential to fast-tracking your 7 Figure Club Success.
>
> Proper measurement of what drives your results is possibly the most important aspect of achieving your big business goal.

The Big Goal — A 7 Figure Club Owner sets the tone and vision with one *Big Goal*.

Clarity of your objective is essential. One of the most common errors made is having multiple Big Goals. Yes, there will be many important objectives. The fact is, there will be plenty of challenges and distractions competing for your time and resources. Pick one big goal, maybe two.

Any more than that and your own big goals will become a distraction, thus neutralizing what you are looking to achieve.

Avoid the landmines that sabotage growth

Landmine 1: Not having all team members working on the same big goal.

If you asked all your employees what the big goal was would they all give the same answer? Rarely. It is essential to get everyone on the same page, and defining the objective the same way. As your organization grows, the disparity between what the owner thinks is the main goal, and what the staff thinks is the main goal, widens. The bigger the gap, the harder it is to achieve your big goal.

Landmine 2: Not committed to the same goal.

Is the team more committed to their paycheck than the big goal? Meaning they really are not committed to the big goal. Do they believe in the goal? Are they excited about it? Do they understand why it matters?

Landmine 3: Not holding everyone accountable to moving forward on attaining the big goal in a *clearly measurable way*.

You must be clear on what actions will drive you toward your big goal. Then you must find a way to measure the actions as well as the results that move you toward the big goal.

As a business owner that has the expectation of building a 7 Figure business, and then seeing it grow to the high 7 figures, and possibly even becoming an Elite 8 Figure business, you must continually work on improving those three areas. That is your role as you build the business rather than operate in it.

Chaos will happen

The SWHTF. Count on it. As my dad said, Murphy's Law will always come into effect. And when @*#$%&! happens, urgency will trump all your best plans of working on what is important. Rather than working on what is important and essential to reach the big goal, you will get sucked into the urgency trap. Rather than getting pulled into the vortex of urgency and being forced to play firefighter, your team must be prepared to extinguish the emergency, eliminate the distraction and stay the course of attaining your Big Goal.

You are setting goals and following your action plan to attain those goals. You and the team are in motion, and focused on priorities. Recognize that you can be doing everything right as you cruise along your path of business growth and then despite all your best practices something will go wrong. Mike Tyson famously said, "Everyone has a plan until they get punched in the mouth."

Your success comes down to problem solving. That is part of what is required to hit the big goal. How do you do it knowing there will inevitably be constant distractions, and unknown forms of chaos lurking around various corners?

Daily tasks versus the Big Goal

Daily tasks take time. Everyone tells themselves the story that they don't have enough time.

Your new big goal will require additional effort, additional focus and possibly additional resources. Expect it. It is almost guaranteed to be the case. This means you need to change the way both you and your team work. Everyone needs to stay focused on what matters most. That often means eliminating the old way of doing things. Build a culture of priority actions that eliminate the waste.

That culture starts with you.

You need to know the six most important actions that will drive your results. The list of important actions will be longer than six, but part of your magic as the leader of the business will be to define the SIX areas of focus that create 90% of the results. I call those "The Big Six."

As you lead by example, you can guide your team to continually focus on the six action areas that will drive 90% of their departments' results too.

> **PRO TIP:** Define the Big Six in terms that can be specifically measured. That distinction is critical in leading your organization to attaining the Big Goal.

> **PRO TIP:** As the leader you must also watch out for the new "shiny object" or "next great opportunity" that will distract the organization from your big goal. Part of Steve Jobs' genius at Apple was keeping the team focused on the Big Goal. One of the things Jobs said he was most proud of was all the things he decided not to create. For each big idea Apple pursed, there were countless other great ideas that were put on the shelf so resources and attention could stay concentrated and focused.

The Accountability Game

Games are more fun when you know the score. To know the score, you need a scoreboard and a way to keep score. Without a scoreboard it is not a game. It's a scrimmage, a practice game where nobody knows if they won. In business that is unacceptable.

PILLAR 2: Accountability

You also need to know *what* you are going to score.

Focus on drivers over results. Most business owners and managers have it backwards. They are focused on a) revenues, b) the bottom-line profit or c) a growth matrix (such as percentage of market share). Sure, you want those numbers to be healthy, but the health of those results is based on specific and measurable actions. To achieve the results, you *must measure* those actions that will drive you toward them.

Select your drivers and measure them

When you know the right drivers to measure you can predict the results with an extremely high level of accuracy.

One of the easiest ways to grasp this is by looking at sales numbers. Most business owners and sales managers keep looking at the annual, quarterly, and occasionally monthly, and in some cases weekly sales numbers. In each case nothing can be done to change the results of those numbers.

Results numbers are old. Driver numbers are fresh and current.

> **PRO TIP:** If you look at numbers **annually**, you can have a bad year, and it is too late to change anything. When you look at numbers **quarterly**, you might have a bad quarter but you can take corrective action to save the year. If you look at the numbers **monthly** you can significantly increase the odds of having a good quarter. Stack those quarters together and suddenly the year is looking really good. And if you are measuring each week, you can do what is needed to have a good month even in spite of a bad week. Your awareness allows you to take appropriate action early. That makes you almost certain to have a great year and at a minimum, guarantees no surprises.

> **PRO TIP:** Be consistent with your tracking. Measure early and often. For it to really count, it must be done in writing. You must be able to see in a clear, readable format.

More important than your result stats are your driver stats. If you are clear on your driver stats you can guide your outcome. This will significantly increase the likelihood of achieving the desired results stat. Knowing your sales drivers and improving them will essentially guarantee your sales results improve.

Accurately Predict Sales Results

Sales are the lifeblood of every organization. They are the fuel for growth. Sales drivers predict sales results.

Rather than looking at the sales *results* which are a picture of what happened in the past, let's look at the sales drivers that tell us what is happening in the present.

The actions that drive sales

1) We need to find new prospects
2) We need to reach out to prospects
3) We need to have presentations with our prospects
4) We need to create proposals based on those presentations

If each of these four sales drivers improved week over week, month over month, how much would you bet that the sales RESULTS will be higher? It would be worth a large wager because you could almost guarantee it would happen.

If you had to choose between tracking *driver stats* which show where your organization is in real time, or *results stats* which are a snapshot of the past, choose the driver stats every time. They will show you what is working and what needs fixing.

Of course tracking both is important — but break the old habit of tracking results instead of drivers.

The sports world illustrates the accuracy of predicting outcomes based on drivers over results:

Picture yourself arriving at a baseball game during the fourth inning and you want to know the score. You turn to the scoreboard and you can't see the number of runs because the lights are out on that section of the scoreboard. However, you can see the section that shows the number of hits and errors. Can you guess which team is winning with a fairly high level of accuracy based on those "driver" stats, rather than the "results" stats of number of runs scored?

Let's say:

Team A has 10 hits compared to Team B only having 2 hits

Team A has made zero errors while Team B has made two errors

If you were asked which team was winning you could easily predict it was team A. If you were asked if the game was close or if team A was leading by a wide margin you would likely think team A had a healthy lead.

Let's say you were watching a football game.

At half time:

Team A has 50 yards rushing and Team B had 97 rushing yards.

Team A has 158 yards passing compared to Team B with 278 passing yards.

Again, based on the above "driver" stats it would be easy to predict the "result" stat of points scored.

But let's look more closely at the passing results for Team A which is struggling here.

The coaches also see that:
- There were 5 dropped passes
- There were 2 blocked passes
- The quarterback was knocked down 2 times
- They had to scramble 4 times
- Etc.

Based on this data, the coaching staff would see a variety of things that need fixing.

The data are "drivers" that tell them what is working and what needs fixing.

> **PRO TIP:** Your big result is influenced by drivers that need to be measured. Often those drivers are the "RESULT" of other drivers that may also be appropriate to measure.

When a stat is measured it improves

You need to keep score and everyone needs to know the score.

First, you need to define what results you want, and then figure out which drivers have the greatest impact on improving the results desired. Then we need to keep track in writing, and post the results so the entire team knows the score.

In my digital agency, we had a 10' by 10' wall dedicated to stats. It was our BIG scoreboard, and each department contributed to it.

There was a set of stats for the SEO department, which tracked the results of onsite organic traffic, but above that *results stat* we also posted how many new pages of content were created and posted, quantity of link building outreach, number of pages optimized, etc. When each of those *driver stats* was strong, the result stats for organic traffic volume, and number of keywords ranking high always climbed.

Our agency's customer service department defined happy customers by the number of reviews they gave us and the ratings of those reviews. However, above those results-stats the team had their driver-stats posted. The team could clearly see that proactively reaching out to clients was important. So each week they made outbound quality control calls to ensure everything was spot on and, if not, learned what was needed to make it right.

They also tracked how frequently they asked for reviews each week. The act of proactively asking how they could make good even better always boosted the average star ratings. The act of asking also boosted the number of reviews received. Again, it was improving each of those drivers that led to improving their "Big Department Goal" which was more 5-star reviews (their result stat).

Know each department's drivers, track those drivers, and results improve.

There were several things that improved staff engagement and accountability as well. Rather than telling them what result needed to be tracked, and which drivers they needed to focus on, we had them brainstorm it. When what was being tracked was *their idea,* their commitment to improving it increased. The level of importance rose; they took more pride in achieving the results. Departments even developed a bit of a rivalry. They each wanted to show that they were on an uptrend thus doing their part to impact our overall big company-wide goal.

They also had to physically post the weekly updates themselves. They had to connect the dots from the previous week. This had them physically drawing the line going up, flat, or down. They were charting the actual trend.

Everyone knew how they were doing. They were literally and figuratively connected to the result.

The workweek wasn't completed until stats were submitted and posted on a Friday afternoon. Winners like to know their numbers. Winners like to show off their uptrend. They are proud of it. It satisfies the human need for significance. When numbers look good, folks like the recognition. When numbers are neutral or weak it gives them a heads-up before there is a significant problem. It also allows them to get the support, resources, or attention they need to help them improve.

> **PRO TIP:** Winners want to know the score. If someone does not like being accountable to their numbers, you have a potential problem. If they don't take pride in their numbers you have an even bigger problem.

Thinning the herd

When the numbers are weak, the writing is on the wall. In our case both literally and figuratively. If someone was not able to improve their drivers, they knew it. That meant they were not getting the desired result. If they could not improve it was clear it was time to go. There was no hiding. They knew it was time to leave, and often would choose the door before being shown the door. If you have put the time and effort into helping someone improve and they can't get the required result, you don't want them on the team, or at least not in that particular role. It is not fair to anyone. It is not fair to them, you, or the rest of the team.

Another client, Chris, also had a digital agency and the desire to scale his business. He sold marketing services in the medical community to independent doctors' offices and

PILLAR 2: Accountability

small medical groups. He had an abundance of prospects to pursue. More than he could reach on his own. When he had the opportunity to hire some highly experienced sales reps he was thrilled to get them.

Unfortunately, the only big sale they were capable of closing was getting Chris to hire them. The two reps were pros. Each had a history of being the top rep at their prior firm, so Chris was willing to be patient. When results were poor and their sales performance weak, he tolerated their reasons for the slow start. He felt lucky to have these superstars. He didn't want to let them go even though the market was soft and their sales low because conferences were being cancelled due to Covid-19.

The results were telling him it wasn't working but he kept giving them more time. He made excuses for them, and understood each rep's justification for weak sales numbers.

When we came in to review the reps' performance, the only number being tracked was sales results. They were low but there were reasons for it that were out of everyone's control and Chris knew if he let these reps go he couldn't get them back. Instead of looking at the results and listening to the tale the reps were spinning about market conditions that were limiting their performance, we had Chris shift his focus to tracking the driver stats.

Several of the key drivers were how many offices were called, how many doctors were spoken to and how many presentations were made. These supposed superstars had dismal numbers on call volume, getting past gate keepers, and when they did have a presentation they had only an average closing percentage.

What the drivers pointed out with bright clarity was that these "superstars" were not even doing the work required to fill their sales presentation pipeline.

The marketplace didn't shrink, but what was required to reach the marketplace had changed. What was required to drive sales had changed, and these so-called superstars did not take the required actions.

When conferences halted, the reps needed to proactively reach out to the doctors. Once the required driver actions started to be measured, and those stats were posted weekly it was obvious the reps were not doing what was needed to fill the pipeline. When low and flat "driver" numbers were visually graphed, and posted each week, the charts clearly posted and painted the picture that was literally there for everyone to see.

Before it was even required to tell the sales representatives that they were not working out (a hard conversation for many business owners), the sales reps already knew it. They could explain the market conditions, but they could not explain a continued lack of adequate driver actions.

The evidence was posted for all to see and the superstar reps resigned quickly. The driver stats saved the firm a significant sum of money.

Driver stats tell you, the team members and the individual, whether things are working.

Tracking stats provide clear evidence to everyone involved on whether a role is the right fit. If things *aren't* working and can't be corrected via training or additional support, it is time to make a personnel shift.

Defining and using driver stats can help an individual or an organization achieve any goal more quickly. It will also make it clear if the parties are serious about attaining the objective or merely talking a big game. Driver and results stats are relevant for each and every area where you want to see significant improvement.

Master the skill of knowing which drivers to track and you master achieving the desired result of any goal more rapidly.

A student says they want the result of improving a particular grade: Drivers are study time and homework assignments completed.

Someone wants to write a book: Drivers are time spent writing daily/weekly, and the number of words written.

Drivers shine a spotlight on the actual performance of each role in real time.

You get what you tolerate

If you tolerate weak performance and weak action on your drivers, you will get weak results.

Even more costly is the damage created when you demotivate your stronger players. Why should they put in all the extra effort if you are willing to tolerate mediocrity?

As the business owner it is your responsibility to set a new higher standard. A higher standard for yourself. A higher standard for the team. A higher standard for the organization. Solidify your new standard by creating the stats scoreboard for all to see.

What Story Does Your Scoreboard Tell You?

The old adage "A picture is worth a thousand words" is so true. When it comes to the health of your business the story is told via the picture of your stats.

You can know volumes in an instant by looking at your stats visually. We don't want to rely only on spreadsheets. Spreadsheets require analysis and calculation. Numbers on a spreadsheet lack emotion. The visual shown in a graph or bar chart communicates a trend and tells a story. What story does your graph communicate?

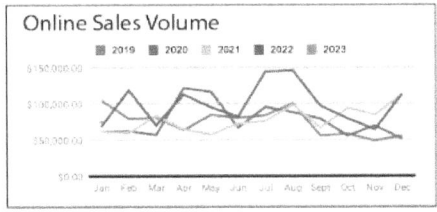
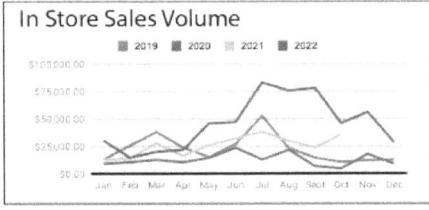
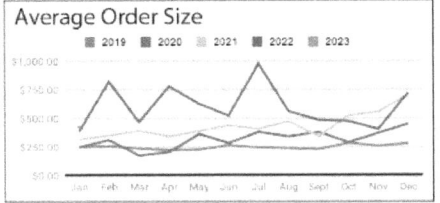
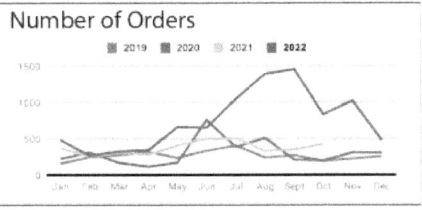

PRO TIP: You can spend hours reviewing spreadsheets or get the full picture in minutes looking at your dashboard graphs.

Install Your Stats Dashboard

Your stats dashboard is your instrument panel. Without it, you are flying blind. You and your business are constantly navigating a wide array of forces. Sometimes it is blue skies and the wind is at your back. Other times you will face fierce marketplace headwinds along with other elements that can be treacherous to profitability and the execution of your plan's success.

A pilot has a comprehensive instrument panel to manage the plane and navigate to the desired destination. The stats dashboard is your instrument panel for managing your business and navigating your way to 7 figures. It will allow you to know if everything is functioning perfectly, or if an adjustment needs to be made somewhere. Sometimes the adjustments will be small tweaks and other times major corrective action will be required to get back on course.

We have assigned meaning to the direction of each stat. By understanding what each trendline means you can better oversee the business. When you connect an emotional meaning to the trend, you and the team will be motivated to quickly correct weak stats and will take great pride in maintaining strong stats that lead to powerful departments and a profitable business that is growing rapidly.

A nosedive needs to be corrected as fast as possible. Everyone knows this. Everybody knows it is unacceptable and can't be tolerated.

On the other hand, a powerful thriving stat is one that everyone takes pride in. They want to be associated with being powerful, improving, and thriving.

Lead with urgency. Grow rapidly. Grow profitably!

> **PRO TIP:** If you are serious about getting your life back by being the owner of your business rather than the operator of the business, the stats dashboard is one of your most essential tools. It's how you know the condition of each department and the overall health of your business. It gives you clear evidence as to how people and departments are functioning. *The stats dashboard is not optional.* It is a *requirement* to your owning, rather than operating a business.

Educate your staff on what trend the stat is communicating. Is the stat healthy or does it show weakness? When they understand the meaning and can read the signs, your team can begin to take ownership of the stat. That allows them to take ownership of their results. This empowers them to be accountable. In turn, it empowers you to own a business and frees you from the ranks of the self-employed.

Reading Your Stats Dashboard

You must know what each trendline is and what action complements each trend in order to effectively use the Stats Dashboard to both increase accountability and empower your team to stay on the 7 Figures Fast Track.

Invisibility — the trouble with zeros

When you have a chart full of zeros, you don't even have a *bleep* or a *blip*. Track it anyway. It is important to know you are at zero even though that is probably not where you want to be. If you can't see it, it is invisible. You literally have nothing to show for your efforts.

In most cases, that is because NOT enough effort or attention has been put into the area that is showing zero.

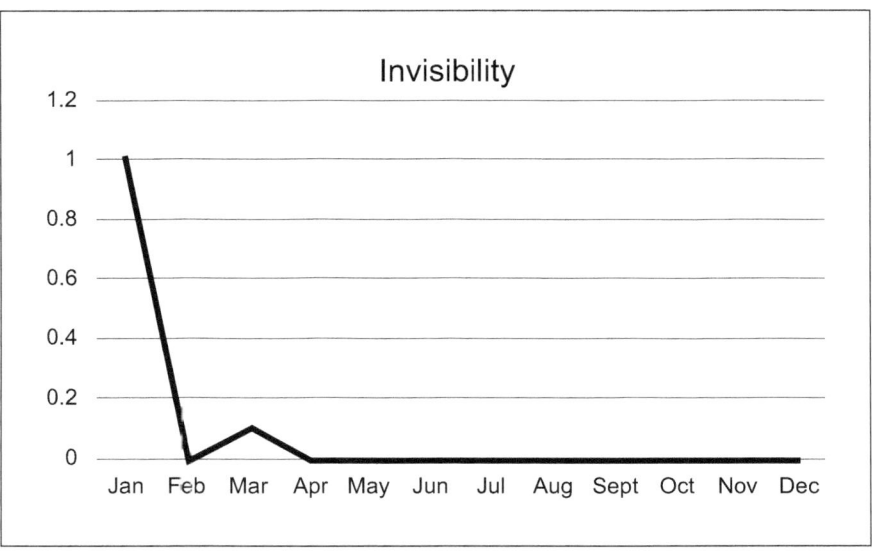

If effort has been put into the area being tracked and you have zeros, that is important information. If you clearly see that nothing has been created from that effort you at least have the benefit of awareness. You need to see this and be confronted by it. Decide if you want to bring this area of your business into existence or if you are fine with it remaining *invisible* and lifeless.

No Substance

When you have the most minimal of numbers showing that you are barely a hair above invisibility, you need to come to terms with the fact that this area of your business is generating a level of effort or results that are insignificant. There is no substance to what is being generated. Assuming this area of your business is meaningful, you need to take appropriate corrective action. Otherwise you have a big gaping hole, and opportunity will vanish.

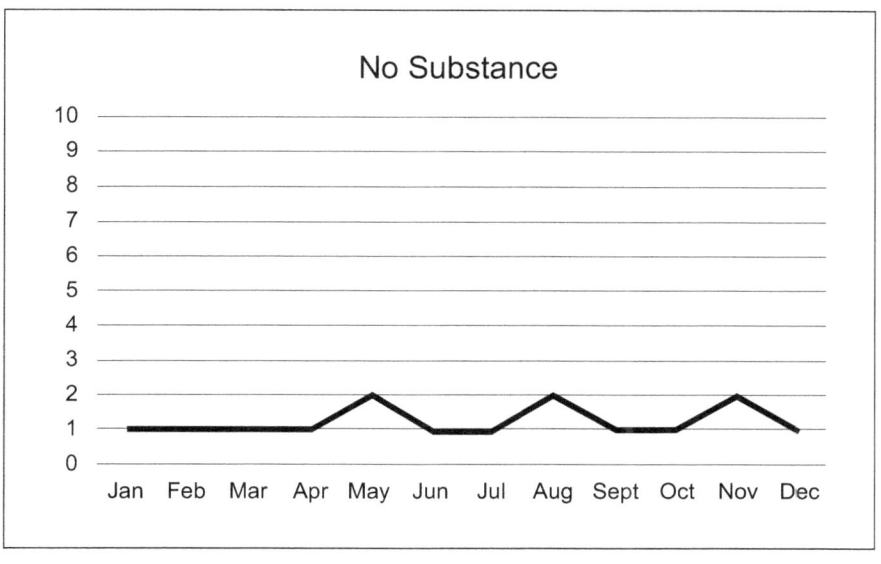

Nosedive

If you have a department or sector of your business that has been cruising along and suddenly the numbers take a nosedive, you have a problem. It could be momentary turbulence or it could be critical. In an airplane, a momentary dip caused by turbulence has you buckle up for a short time. The pilot navigates through it and you're back to enjoying your meal or movie — business as usual.

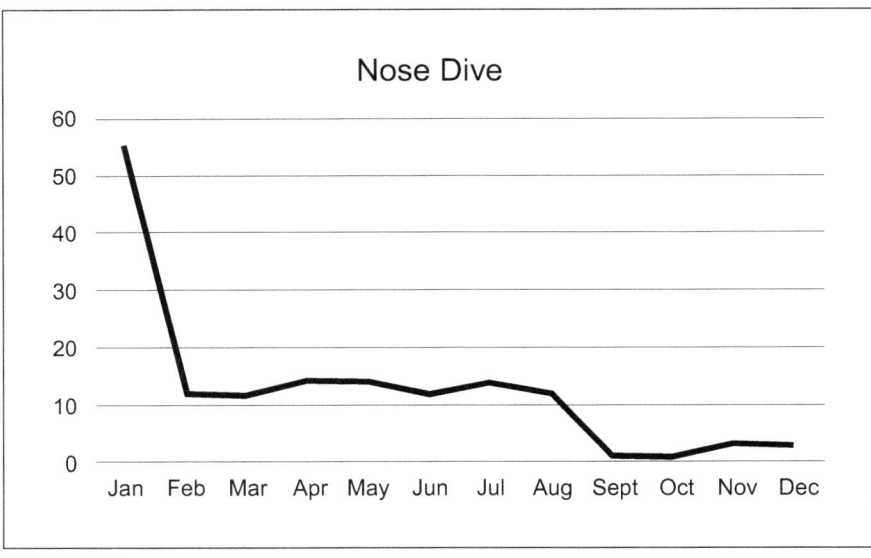

If the nosedive is not corrected, you have an emergency. You need to know this, otherwise you can dip below a critical level, one in which you may not be able to recover. A prolonged downward dip is an emergency. Address it fast. Correct it fast. This is not the time for patience or observing the trend. The faster an emergency is noticed and addressed, the easier it is to correct. Damage will be minimized. Ignore the emergency and your *nosedive* will quickly turn into a tailspin from which you may never recover.

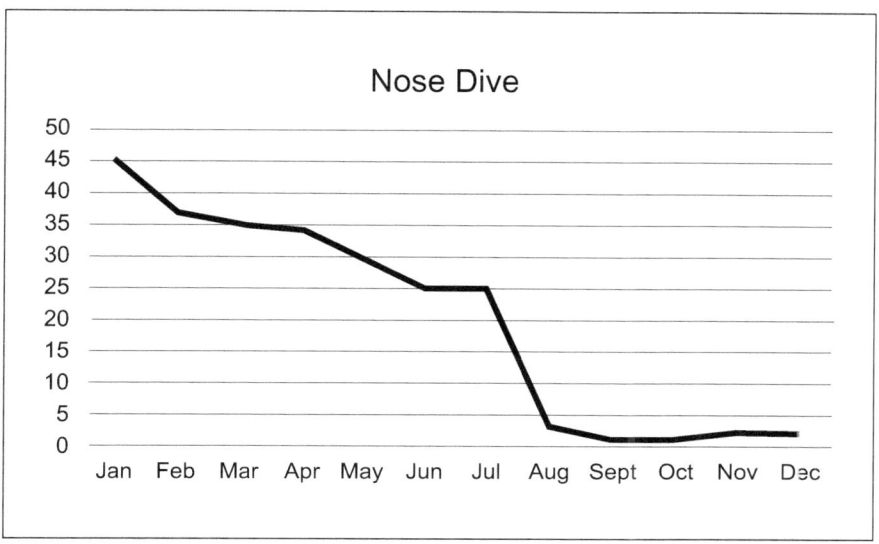

You must acknowledge a prolonged nosedive. Yes, crummy stats suck. They're depressing. They're embarrassing. They make everybody want to hide in the corner.

Ignoring all that discomfort is totally unacceptable. Even worse is not even knowing the extent of your prolonged downward slide because you failed to track the trend. That is NEGLIGENCE.

Course Correction

When you see your trendline shifting *downward* it is time for a course correction.

A course correction is a minor dip where a stat continues to steadily decline. Unlike the nosedive where the drop is rather sudden, this decline is gradual. Because of this it is often unnoticed. Even when it is noticed many business owners and managers fail to take corrective action because they did not know that the corrective action was essential.

Learn to rely on your stats dashboard. It is your instrument panel. Without it the odds of accurately knowing where you are is very low. When going after any goal, especially your big goal, you will continually need to make adjustments.

Most business owners do not monitor departments and people consistently. It is even rarer that they know the specifics in a timely fashion.

The faster you spot a trend, the faster you can work with it.

If you see your trendline going down fix it early when all that is needed are some modifications aka basic *course corrections*. If you ignore the downward trendline, you may see the situation deteriorate into a nosedive.

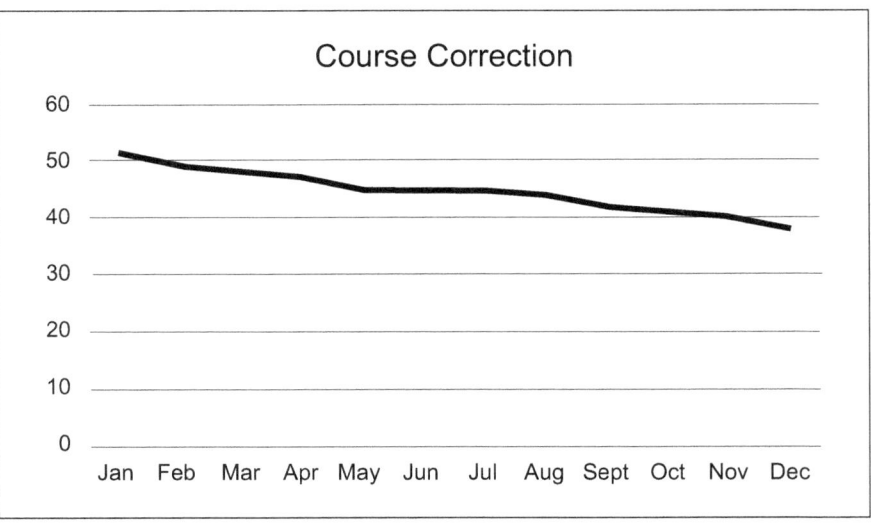

Every downward trend is not going to turn into an emergency. What does happen VERY frequently is that *weak stats persist for far too long*. If you have a weak unhealthy stat and it is clearly visible and monitored weekly, or monthly, it is much more likely that it will be repaired quickly rather than tolerated. Often the greatest loss is that of lost opportunity. Take action to direct the course to that of opportunity rather than let weeks turn into months in which the time can never be recovered.

Indifference aka Flat Line Stats

Why do we refer to the flat line stat as *indifference* rather than neutrality? A flat line is one that is not going up. It is not improving. Is that an acceptable condition as a business owner?

Our entrepreneurial nature is one of growth, improvement and problem-solving. We should not be content with neutral. If you are excepting the neutral flat line, consider that you may actually be treating the area with a flat line stat with indifference.

I remember a saying I heard years ago. *The opposite of love is not hate, it is indifference.* That was profound. Interestingly enough, that mindset can be applied to business. The opposite of everything flying higher in your business is not low sales, it is indifference.

Both high sales and growth, along with bumps in the road, are filled with emotion, action, and a heightened awareness to what is going on in the business.

Indifference is the opposite. It is lack of awareness, a lack of connection, and being disconnected. Each is a serious concern to the long-term growth of your business. When you notice your business and your business stats in a state of indifference it is time to take a careful look at what needs attention.

As the owner, you are the proverbial Captain of the Ship. Make sure you know what your flat line means. Is your flat line at a level of complacency, acceptance, or excellence?

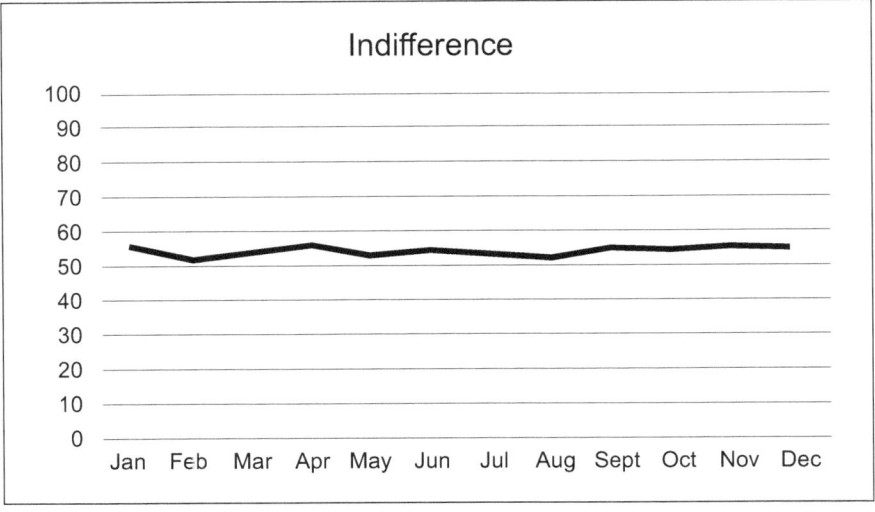

Take a look at the area. What attention should you be giving to that department? Are there areas where minimal effort could take something that is good and make it even better? Sometimes a flat stat is at such a high-performance level it merely needs to be maintained. Other times the flat line is at a level where we are accepting "*good* is good enough."

PRO TIP: Small businesses often have limited resources. Sometimes we may accept a flat line because of the limited availability of resources, meaning time, money, or staffing, which need to be focused on a correction of a weaker stat. This temporarily allows us to accept the area that is "flat."

Blue Skies — An Opportunity to Climb Higher

When your trendline is steadily going upward, things are heading in the right direction. People and departments are functioning nicely. If you maintain this pace, you will see the business and each department continue to get stronger.

PILLAR 2: Accountability

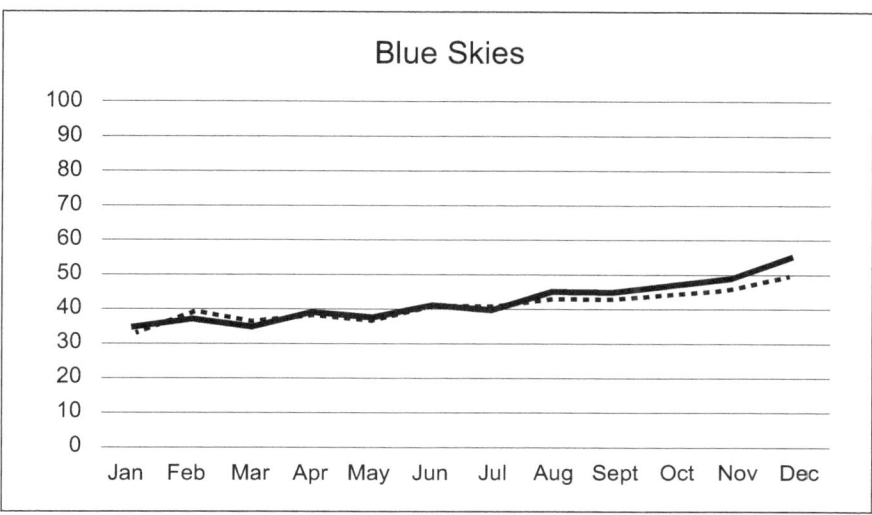

Identify what is working. Acknowledge it. Duplicate it. Praise the people responsible for it. And definitely continue doing what is working, so you maintain it.

When things are trending upwards that is good. We also need to know whether we are at our best. Just because a stat is moving up it does not mean it is as high as it could be. Are we maximizing the opportunity in front of us? Are we maximizing our potential?

Are we moving forward at the right pace? Are we on schedule or should we be getting more done, more quickly?

PRO TIP: You and the team need to know where they are going and when they expect to be there. In terms of stats this means we also need to plot projections (illustrated as a dotted line) for each driver and result stat. Do this at the start of the year or at the start of each quarter. Pre-plotting the projection line is essential because as time goes on your solid black line shows whether you are above the dotted projection line (excellent), right on schedule or veering off course.

> **PRO TIP:** If you have prior-years' data, continue to show those too. This allows you to plan for seasonal trends and better interpret trends. Strive to improve year over year for the same time period.

Abundance — The Upward Hockey Stick

Our favorite stat and space to be living in is that of abundance. Whether it is sales, cash flow or improved fitness, we love when the numbers are moving upward quickly and steeply. When you track your numbers, you are striving for your drivers to be in a state of abundance. Abundant driver stats create abundant result stats. Strive to have that upward hockey stick jump.

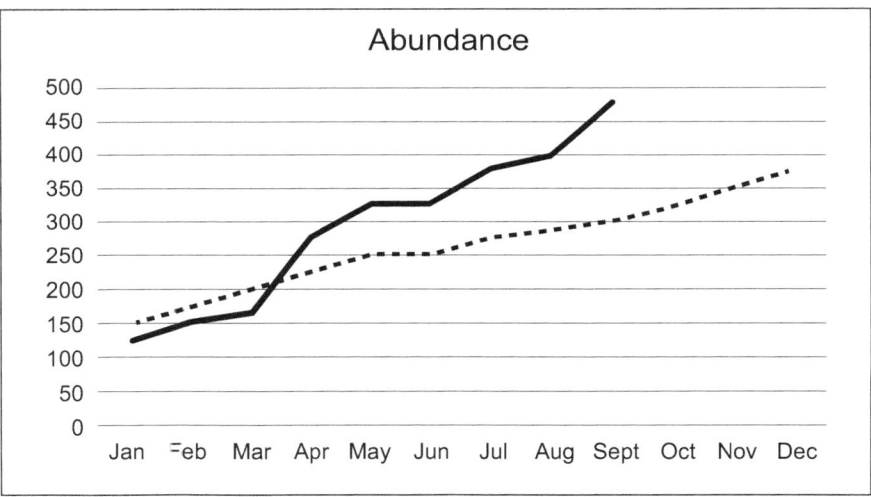

As much as we love abundance it is also sort of like dessert. For many it is their favorite part of the meal, but can't be sustained forever. The hockey stick upward spike gets you to a new higher standard.

> **PRO TIP:** When in a state of abundance, enjoy the ride, and keep doing what is working. This is not the time to make big new changes. Stay on your winning track and enjoy winning!

BASE CAMP

This is an interesting stat, although your state of abundance has flattened out it is far from indifference. You have found a new level of excellence upon which you can build.

When a stat is at a new high, and maintained, it levels off. Although it might appear to be flattening out, it is important to recognize this is natural. That new level you have reached is a new plateau. A new higher high. I like to think of this as "Base Camp."

It is an accomplishment to get to the high levels of base camp. Base camp is not a comfortable resting-place. Base camp is the place where you adjust to your new higher levels of achievement. It is a new resting-place as we prepare for summiting a new higher level of peak performance. You continue to get stronger, take stock in your success and prepare for the next move upward. This is not a place of complacency.

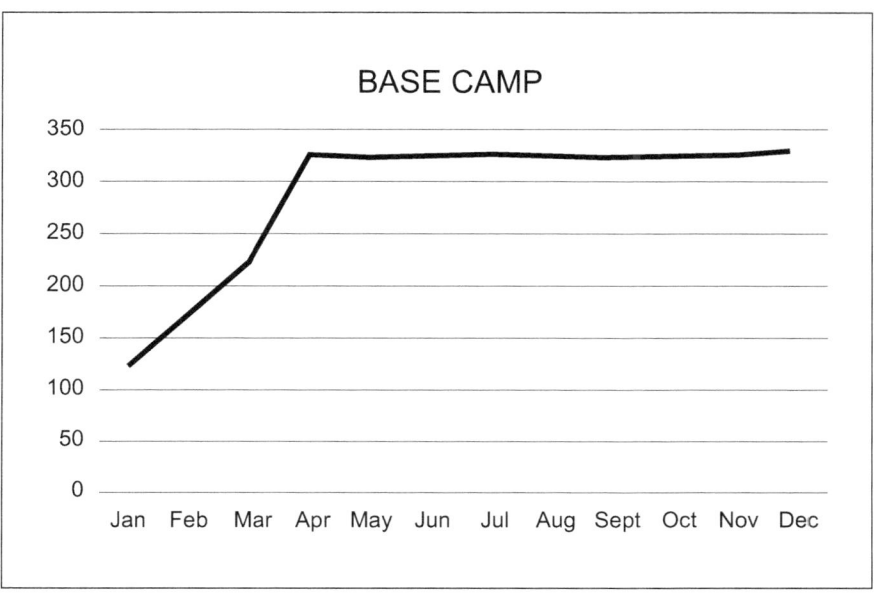

Base Camp is a tricky and sensitive location. Climbing higher has risks and it also has the potential for great rewards. If you are not cautious, you can get careless and use resources inappropriately. You can get overzealous and take on challenges you were not ready for. You need to check in at Base Camp. Confirm that each aspect of the business is solid, stable and healthy. Then you can continue to build on a new solid foundation. Keep climbing higher, but when you do level off make sure each department is stable and healthy in order to establish a new operating standard.

Summary

Only 1 in 10 business owners achieves 7 figures in sales. Only 1 in 10 Americans achieve a 7-figure net worth, and even fewer in other parts of the world. My friend Jon Carroll, the former President of Spanx, made an interesting observation that fewer than 1 in 10 business owners have a stats dashboard. When he mentors business leaders the emphasis on stats and a visible dashboard is huge. He continually preaches that it is an essential building block, and required for any business to truly scale.

Whether you are overseeing a billion-dollar brand such as Spanx or you're CEO of your own 7 Figure Club Business, your role as a leader is to have each department on track with its drivers. If you want 7 and 8 figure sales revenues as well as higher profits, your dashboard is the foundation. Once it is in place you can build your sales process and watch the sales climb higher.

PILLAR 3
SALES — GET MORE FASTER

Without a high volume of sales, no business survives or thrives

If you want a high stat of profitability then you need a huge sales stat too. One that far exceeds your expenses. Therefore, your success in business is tied directly to sales. Make lots and lots of sales and you succeed. Do a million or more in sales and you become one of the 1 in 10 that make it into the 7 Figure club.

Sales is easy. Most people overcomplicate it. Keep it simple.

The 7 Figures Sales Formula

When you have a rep that treats sales time as a priority and consistently spends the required time connecting with prospects you have the potential for sales excellence. But time spent pursuing prospects without a proven sales process will frustrate your rising stars. On the other hand, another profit pitfall is the gifted sales person, the natural closer that fails to put in the hours to prospect and pursue each lead. They are doing the minimum it takes to look good, and that will cost you a fortune in lost opportunity.

Evaluate each of your sales reps efforts, and recognize which quadrant their effort and skills place them in.

Where would you place each member of your sales team? Who is a rising star that needs their skills to be nurtured? Who is a lead-killer that needs to be cut? Who is wasting their potential and needs to be challenged to step up? Who is a Sales Superstar that needs to be celebrated?

You must manage and motivate your sales team to have BOTH their sales time and sales skills be at a level 7 or higher. As a business owner who expects 7 Figure Results it is your responsibility to manage the revenue drivers of time spent selling and the closing skills of your team.

> **PRO-TIP:** Solid Sales Skills + Significant Time Selling = Superstar Sales Success

90% of Your Sales Success Can Be Learned from a Seven-Year Old

Many people said I was a natural-born salesperson. Funny, I never thought of it that way. As a kid I was shy, but I was also entrepreneurial. At the age of seven, I started on one of my first "business" endeavors. It was recycling

PILLAR 3: Sales

newspapers. I learned that the scrap yard would give you a penny for each pound of paper brought to the recycling plant. That created an instant and attainable goal: Collect 100 pounds of newspapers from the neighbors, and I would get 1 dollar.

I didn't even weigh anywhere near 100 pounds myself, but that wouldn't deter me from collecting 100 pounds of recycled newsprint. I grabbed my little red wagon from the garage and set out knocking on my neighbor's doors. They either happily gave me what they had in old newspapers or said "Come back in a week and we will have a bundle waiting for you."

I realized that asking only 10 neighbors would not get me the result I needed, so I made a point to knock on EVERY door on each side of the block. I went up one end of the street and then down the other. I knocked on each front door, side door, and even made sure I gave people time to get to the door. And if there was no answer I went back the next day.

After all, I had to get as many people as possible to save those old papers if I was to reach my 100-pound quota.

On the first go around, I collected 40 or so pounds from the folks who had some old papers ready to toss. But the following Saturday — look out. I came a knockin', and a bunch of them had papers ready for me. Those who didn't were shocked that a little kid actually followed up. I gave them a sad little face and they assured me they would have papers for me the following week.

I assured them I would be back and like clockwork the following Saturday there I was. I hit everyone's door again. Folks knew I was coming, they were ready, and I was too. Boy was my wagon full. A 67-pound kid pulling a big haul on his wagon. I'm not sure who was more excited each week, the neighbors or me.

Oh, and at the weigh-in at the recycling plant, I learned the results of all that labor.

I had exceeded my goal and almost doubled my weight in paper capacity. The owner of the recycling plant handed me $1.26 and I still remember how proud I was. Still remember dad's face too. He jokes about how he spent more money on gas driving me to the recycling plant than I made. But the lessons learned were worth a fortune.

It is amazing how many business lessons that experience taught me and that I was fortunate enough to grasp them at such a young age.

These are lessons every business owner needs to apply, whether they are a natural-born sales person or someone who claims sales isn't their thing even though they are in business.

The Three Big Lessons

It is so simple. I knew my prospects (the neighbors) and I asked each of them for the order (hold their papers for me). And then I kept asking, again and again. That was the First Big Lesson.

The Second Big Lesson: Clarity of my goal. I had a specific target to easily judge my progress and results.

The Third Big Lesson is the biggest sales lesson of them all: Sales is a NUMBERS GAME.

You need to "present" to numerous prospects. If you only ask a few, and focus only on those that are convenient you will fall short. Some folks who I thought would surely hold their papers for me each week didn't, and others surprised me with more than expected — even bringing papers from their office to give to me.

> **PRO TIP:** SALES IS A NUMBERS GAME. Always remember that. Keep asking a large quantity of qualified prospects for the order and you will succeed. FOLLOW UP MULTIPLE TIMES.

Sales for the Non-Salesperson

If you are reading this book, you are likely a business owner and definitely someone who has ambition and the desire to succeed. Regardless of your comfort level with sales, you can surely do everything a 7-year old boy did. Define your prospect, and offer your services to them.

I'm going to make it so easy that even if you don't like sales or say "I hate selling" you will become someone who can communicate the massive value your product or service offers to others. That is the core principle that allowed me to help thousands of other business owners and their team members succeed in sales.

THE SECRET: If you focus on the **other** person's needs rather than your goal of a sale, you will succeed.

Avoid the #1 Selling Mistake

The biggest mistake most salespeople make when they get in the door is that they rush in to tell their prospect about their product. They have so much product knowledge and they are eager to share it. They are so excited and enthusiastic to share that they forget the most important thing and that is to uncover what need is MOST IMPORTANT to the prospect.

This is a massive mistake because you can't sell unless you understand what your prospect needs. Learning what the prospect needs is the most crucial element required in order to convince a prospect that you are someone they can trust and work with. WITHOUT knowing what is *most important to the prospect* you can't target your presentation to what is most important to them. You might get lucky, and address their main need because you know your market place, but that is far less effective than getting the prospect to admit it to you.

People buy to solve their main needs. Qualified prospects buy quickly when their most important needs are satisfied. *You must make sure you ask them, "What is most important to you?"*

> **PRO TIP:** After asking the prospect what is most important to them, follow up by asking the question, "How do you define that?" Typically when salespeople ask the first question they get a rather general answer such as a desire to increase profits, get a good ROI, to have a great experience, to look good, etc. Ask the prospect to define the result they are looking for based on their general answer. Then in your presentation show them how that will be achieved via your product or service.

After asking well-thought-out questions, actually *stop* and *listen* to the answer. Really hear what your prospect shared.

Listening to your customers and establishing rapport will enable you to discover their needs, and thus provide them the most suitable solution to their problem. The connection you establish makes it easier for prospects to really open up. Even if you knew their specific need, getting the prospect to admit it in their own words is essential. When they say it out loud to you they are also outwardly reaffirming the need to themselves.

You and your reps should always be friendly and genuinely interested in what the prospects have to say. Reps should not only try to sell, they should also focus on developing relationships.

Remember, all things being equal, people do business with people they like. Even when products or services are not equal, business is still more often than not done with people they like.

> **PRO TIP:** Offering a service is not enough. You must state your offer and position your services in a way that fills the need that your prospect has expressed. When you can position yourself as someone who is serving the specific need expressed by the prospect, you become much more essential to the customer.

The Right Questions F.U.E.L. Profitability

When you get in front of a qualified prospect you must get them excited about what you have to say. To do this we are going to be a bit untraditional. The focus will NOT be on our product or service and how great it is. Instead we will get the prospect to tell us why they need us, why they want us and why they would prefer to buy from us rather than our competitors.

People love to buy and hate to be sold. *By asking the right questions the prospect becomes a buyer rather than someone you are selling.* This is a crucial to your sales success and developing a sales process that works for you.

Your sales process must be based on pre-planning which questions you will ask. This allows you to duplicate your best sales presentations. It allows you to consistently get a prospect excited about your product by having the conversation relate to *them* rather than your product. When your sales process has specific and structured questions that create a friendly connection, and within the first few minutes has the prospect admitting their needs and what desire will be satisfied by buying your product the sales number climb higher quickly.

Your job is to uncover their needs. Do that and you succeed. Put anything ahead of this and you will struggle to Join The 7 Figure Club.

Just ask the right questions, listen to the answers and then show how buying from you is the solution. That is what sales superstars do. They get the prospect to admit their needs and then talk about solving the needs that were uncovered.

To most effectively hear their needs, put yourself in the prospect's shoes and think about what they really want. It is never the widget you sell. It is the "RESULT" they get from that widget. Listen for the values and experiences your prospect expressed. When you can satisfy your prospect's values and you can envision the experience they want delivered via working with you, you can start creating a sales presentation that has a high probability of closing.

> **PRO TIP:** If you have a partial- or non-decision maker you are not trying to sell them your product. The sale you are going for is to sell them on putting you in front of the decision maker. Superstars know the info gatherer will never fully communicate value, so the goal is to have them put you in front of the decision maker.

PILLAR 3: Sales

QUALIFIED PROSPECT REQUIREMENTS

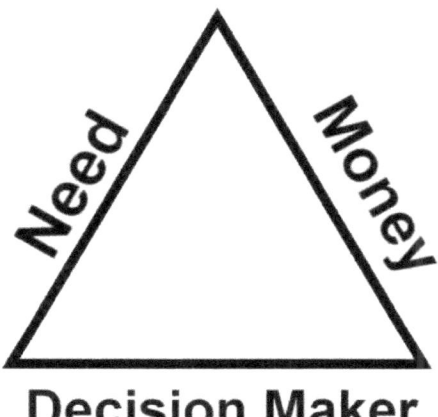

Decision Maker

It is impossible to close an unqualified prospect.

Rookies and struggling reps continually make the mistake of trying to close unqualified prospects.

If any one of the 3 elements is missing, the prospect will not buy.

The #1 Way to Close More Sales

When you uncover the prospect's needs by asking questions you become a trusted advisor and consultant. *Consultative selling is the easiest way to close more sales.*

Being consultative takes your sales ability to the next level. It sets you apart from the competition. The easiest way to do that is to ask the right questions.

For example let's look at Craig, one of the salespeople we helped during a sales training at a computer software firm. In a typical day, he would visit four different prospects, all of whom could benefit from his firm's software solutions. Each one will have different perceived needs and goals for enhancing computer systems. His software could in fact satisfy the needs of all four highly qualified prospects, but approaching all four prospects with the same or a similar sales pitch will most likely fail to excite any of them about the purchase.

It definitely won't sell all of them. The objective on a sales call is to find out what each prospect is looking for. You must learn each prospect's unique viewpoint. You need to know what they think is most important, and how they define that. You must be able to present your product in a way that satisfies needs from the prospect's perspective.

Avoid "Fast Food" Selling Approaches

If Craig gave the same sales pitch to all four people, he would be applying the fast-food approach to selling. The presentation would be satisfactory to everyone, but will not excite anyone!

This concept is similar to what you do automatically in your personal life. Look at how you have solved the problems of others throughout your life. You help people with their problems based on what you know about them and their objectives. You address the same problem for different people in different ways.

A reading problem with a child in school would be handled differently depending on whether it was caused by an issue with study habits, a learning disability, or a family problem.

If you think about it, you'll realize that life is full of situations in which you have been effective because you took the time to gather pertinent information about the person you were helping, as well as their situation, so that you could craft a solution specific to them.

Remember, you could not effectively solve the problem without trust, understanding the desired objective, and your specialized knowledge. The same is true for sales.

F.U.E.L.: Find Your Prospect's Unique Need

We solve the #1 mistake of not asking the right questions, and uncovering the prospect's needs, with F.U.E.L. which is my method for developing a relationship with your prospect, uncovering what they need, and leveraging what they desire in order to close the sale.

It stands for four sets of questions:

F is for **Friendship-building** questions.

U is for questions that **Uncover Needs**.

E is asking questions that **Establish** you are in agreement with your prospect.

L is asking questions that give you the **Leverage** to close based on the value and experiences the prospect is looking to gain from your product.

F.U.E.L. is a structured step-by-step system that makes clients feel comfortable and special using regular conversation and problem-solving techniques. To mentally prepare yourself for using F.U.E.L. most effectively on a sales call, don't think of yourself as being there to sell a product.

Your main goal is to solve your clients' needs. This can't be done with a one-size-fits-all pitch. When you go on a sales call you already know your product but you don't know your clients' needs. The key to selling is using your presentation to find out about your prospect's needs. Remember, any time you can truly help the prospect meet their needs you have a reason to close. You should move forward and work together.

F.U.E.L. Makes Closing Easy

- **F**riendly: Create a friendly bond between you and your prospect. The friendly vibe establishes trust and enables you to find out what your prospect is looking for.
- **U**ncover your prospect's needs and concerns.
- **E**stablish yourself as someone who listens to and understands your prospect's needs. This is another crucial step in having prospects feel you are someone they can trust and work with.
- **L**everage your close on their big result desired. Go beyond a prospect's initial statement of objectives and address what results they are really looking for from your product. By tapping into this motivation, you will be able to position yourself as the person to fill those needs and gain a powerful advantage over your competition.

Craig used F.U.E.L. to take his sales skills to a new level. Once he started using F.U.E.L. questions early in his presentation, he set the stage for a higher closing percentage. After some initial pleasantries, he starts to ask questions that uncovered needs rather than sharing information about his products or services.

> **PRO TIP:** Most reps and business owners hurt their closing percentages by talking about their product or service too soon. You are there to help the prospect, not to talk about you and your firm.

The more effort Craig put into developing relations with both prospects and customers the faster his closing percentage improved. He became relationship-focused instead of sales-focused, which quickly led to many more sales. Each time you put the prospect and customer first you take a step toward improving your business and building a foundation for a 7 and 8 figure business.

Notice in the following illustration how Craig warms up to the prospect, uncovers their needs and develops an understanding of the prospect's priorities. He is never pushy. Instead he is always friendly and interested in what the prospect has to say.

F.U.E.L. ILLUSTRATION #1:
Craig's Sales F.U.E.L.

Friendly is the foundation of Trust & Connection

During the first step of F.U.E.L., Craig establishes a friendly connection with an IT services buyer Phillip, who is the IT Manager of a major department store, by asking questions that allowed him to learn about his prospect as an individual:

- How long have you been with this particular department store?
- What brought you to New York?
- How do you like the city?
- How did you get into IT solutions?

As the friendly discussion gains momentum, Phillip opens up to Craig and shares various bits of information that become gems on which to further the connection.

It's at this point that Phillip reveals that he got into IT while going to school in the Midwest. Craig mentioned how he went to Northwestern University, which is also in the Midwest. As they discussed that common ground, a friendly vibe was instantly established.

Never underestimate the power of likeability, personal comfort and familiarity. These things build trust and create a bond between prospect and sales representative. It breaks down the barriers that are present in any sales situation. All things being equal, people will do business with people they like. Things not being equal, they will still do more business with people they like.

Uncover Needs

Once Craig feels he has established rapport with Phillip, he begins asking questions that "UNCOVER" needs:
- Tell me about some of the frustrations tied to using multiple software products to solve your IT problems?
- Share a bit about what problems keep coming up for you in managing the department?
- With all that's going on in your life, what could I do as your direct point person to makes things easier on you?
- What challenges have you had with prior vendors?
- Please explain what is most important to you. Define that a bit more please.

Phillip told Craig that having someone to deal with details, such as expediting work orders and helping review the monthly analysis reports, would make his job easier. Phillip said he would be thrilled if Craig would prepare a summary report that guided him on which items he should make a priority to address. He said he would feel better if Craig would handle follow-up on open items so he wouldn't have to handle that as well.

Purpose: *The reason you ask questions about the difficulties and challenges while uncovering needs is that they teach you what is valuable to your prospect besides price.*

Keep in mind that offering good service is not enough. You must state your offer in a way that fills the need that your prospect has expressed.

When you can position yourself as someone who is serving the specific needs expressed by the prospect, you become much more essential to the prospect. In the case of IT Manager Phillip, the issue of software facts and features is not nearly as important having someone be his liaison with the help desk and eliminating other tedious tasks. By presenting the benefit of great service in the exact way the buyer defines service, Craig dramatically increases his chances of getting the sale.

Establish Agreement To Establish Trust

To establish agreement Craig says: "So if I understand you correctly, what you need from me as your rep is to totally eliminate the communication lags with the help desk, to expedite work orders, and help you spot the big opportunities hidden in the monthly reporting."

Purpose: Craig makes Phillip feel comfortable working with him because he demonstrates that he is someone who understands him and offers the services that are important to him.

Leverage your "close" on their desired result

Once Craig has established to his buyer, Phillip, that he understands what Philip needs, Craig wants to get to the next level and understand what motivates Phillip to want these details handled. The key question here is: What would be the major benefit to you, if I did all these things for you?

Phillip tells Craig if he could do the summary report analysis for him, and if he could primarily deal with Craig, he would no longer have the aggravation of wasting time on hold, and sending countless follow-up emails. He said he wants to stop having to worry about various details, and can be confident each will be taken care of. This would ultimately lead to stress reduction and job security.

Purpose: What Craig finds out is that Phillip wants his life to be more simplified, his stress reduced and his job security enhanced. *By knowing this, Craig knows what motivates Phillip.*

This example illustrates how Craig is selling much more than software and IT services. Craig is selling Phillip on convenience. Craig is selling Phillip on Craig's ability to save Phillip's time.

Friendly vibe questions established the trust; **U**ncovering needs questions exposed the prospect's concerns; the **E**stablishing agreement question built up confidence and trust in Craig and showed that he listened and understood what the prospect really needed.

Lastly, the **L**everage question allowed Craig to learn that Phillip's real motive in working with him is convenience, stress reduction and simplifying things for him.

The reason F.U.E.L. is essential is that in a sales situation there will be many other reps competing with you on price and other features. You have to get the sale by establishing a relationship and showing the prospect you are the representative who really understands their needs.

F.U.E.L. ILLUSTRATION #2:
Closing on the Prospect's Motivation

Tracy is a representative who sells life insurance. In her first year she grossed more than $1,000,000 in sales and has done $1,000,000 or more ever since.

Tracy uses F.U.E.L. very successfully.

On a recent sales call Tracy met with Carlo, a successful recruiting executive in his late twenties, who is single and really on the move with his career. Normally someone like Carlo would be a hard sale for life insurance.

The first thing Tracy did was ask **F**riendship-building questions such as "What a great photo of you on skis." "How did you first get into skiing?" "What are your favorite places for skiing?" "How often do you go?"

Through these questions, Tracy learned that Carlo loves the active lifestyle, that he loves to get a ski house every winter, and that he wants escape weekends to be part of his lifestyle forever, not just his youth. Since she also appreciates skiing, she quickly established the bond of being a young, active professional who appreciates both working hard and playing hard.

She moved into asking about **U**ncovering need questions and gaining clarity on Carlo's difficulties with the statement, "Saving is hard with our active lifestyle." Carlo agreed, and then she asked him what type of structured savings plan he currently followed? Tell me about your biggest frustrations related to saving consistently. What are your biggest concerns with investments? Please tell me about some of the difficulties you have encountered with past investment experiences.

From these questions, she learned he often spends money extravagantly and could easily put more aside and that although his ability to follow a plan has yielded a great reward in business, he admittedly has been less consistent in applying the same amount of discipline in his financial future.

Tracy then Established they were on the same page by asking "If I understand you correctly, you appreciate the importance of a plan."

Carlo agreed this was true and even gave some weak excuses why he wasn't following a plan despite realizing it was important.

Now, *rather than jumping on this opportunity* to sell Carlo a financial plan or life insurance, *Tracy held off*, knowing from Carlo's answer and her experience that this type of prospect does not see the urgency of an insurance plan while single and young. Instead they feel they will always be healthy and making more money.

So she asked: "If you could be handed $1,000,000 in 20 years, where would you get a ski condo? If I could guarantee the result of saving money when you're married, plus have a dream ski condo in 20 years, all without changing your spending patterns, how would this be for you?"

As Carlo described the ski house and fun with his future family, he was convincing himself of why this might be the right time to invest in life insurance.

Tracy now has all the info, and knowledge about Carlo's motivations to create a sale. The foundation is set for the sale. It is now up to her to present facts and benefits about her products and services to show Carlo how his dreams will be moving in the right direction by working with Tracy.

After learning about her prospect's needs, she used those needs as Leverage to close the sale.

Tracy can present her product in a way that gets Carlo to see himself benefiting by doing business with Tracy now.

Why Add F.U.E.L. To Your Presentations

It's the sincere, genuine interest that makes it so effective to combine building a friendly vibe and uncovering the buyer's true needs.

That's one of the tools that separates 7 figure leaders and sales superstars apart from the pack. Remember, all things being equal people do business with friends and people they like. Even when products and services are not equal, business is still more often done with people who are enjoyable to deal with and deliver results.

F.U.E.L. lights the fire of friendship, likeability and rapport.

Prepare Your Own F.U.E.L.

It is important to formally write out the questions you plan on using.

Writing out the questions helps you consistently duplicate your best presentations. It also allows you to create a sales process others can follow which will help scale the business.

The following sample questions will help you create your own special blend of sales F.U.E.L. immediately. Obviously, adjust these questions to fit your personal style, and the situation you are selling in. Use them to form a structured set of "interview questions" that will keep you and your sales team on a path to uncover the buyers needs and leverage the ability to close. Notice how each question uncovers information that can help move the presentation forward. When combined together they consistently improve closing percentages.

Sample Friendly Vibe Building Questions

Likeability, that good feeling right from the start, is the foundation of F.U.E.L. and sets the tone of the presentation.

Your friendly questions get people talking to you. When they talk to you. When they feel they can relate to you, they start to open up, drop their guard, and are more comfortable sharing. They'll begin to feel safe and secure when speaking with you, which will help them share bigger things, such as what they need from your product, and what their ultimate goal is.

These friendly questions build rapport, establish trust and even genuine friendships. The friendly vibe breaks down the defensive wall that naturally exists between prospect and salesperson when they first meet.

Some Questions To Set A Friendly Tone

- How did you get involved in this business?
- What made you choose this location for your business?
- How did you get into this line of work?
- What made you decide to go into your own business?
- I see you're active with your local scout troop. Tell me about your involvement?
- That piece of artwork is exquisite. Why did you start painting/collecting?
- What's the story behind how you selected the business name?
- Based on your accent, you're not from the US. What brought you here?

Uncovering Needs Questions

When in the sales role, your NUMBER ONE objective is to solve your prospect's problems and satisfy their needs.

Do that and the sales follow. Your prospect will buy again and again. Therefore you must Uncover what your prospect's problems and needs are, and make them realize the urgency of their concerns. Although each of your clients may have similar needs you will not know the specifics of each client's situation and how they perceive their most pressing needs unless you ask about their difficulties and problems.

It's crucial to ask a prospect to describe their difficulties to you. Get them to express it in their own words. You may assume you understand their problems, but you may be assuming incorrectly. Only by allowing the prospect to express difficulties themselves can you find out exactly what they need fixed.

> **PRO TIP:** When they are telling you, they are also admitting the issue out loud to themselves!

Sample Uncovering Needs Questions

- What are your biggest difficulties with delivery?
- When it comes to vendors, explain how they dropped the ball in the past?
- Tell me about your greatest concerns related to the competition.
- Why do you feel XYZ Corporation is your greatest competition?
- What obstacles keep prospects from noticing your value versus your competition?

- What is the greatest challenge in getting customers to appreciate all you offer?
- What are several of the biggest problems you have had with suppliers?
- Tell me about the biggest difficulty you are currently facing.
- Establish Agreement & Being on The Same Page

The purpose of getting the prospect to admit you are on the same page, i.e. **E**stablishing Agreement, is twofold: First, it allows you to see if you understand the prospect's main priorities. Second, it shows the prospect you listened and understood them.

These questions are essential because the potential for misunderstanding a prospect's priorities is so great. When you are digging deep to uncover needs the prospect can share many pain points. We want to be sure we know which one is the big one. And getting them to admit which one is their main concern moves you closer to them needing you as their solution.

Only by accurately focusing on what your client needs can you effectively sell to them.

Also, remember that every businessperson is yessed nearly to death by employees, contractors and salespeople who do things incorrectly after they claimed to understand instructions.

When a prospect feels that they are talking to someone who understands them, they will want to work with you.

Sample Establish Agreement Questions

- If I understand you correctly, what you are saying is ____, is that right?
- So your main concerns is ____, isn't it?

- The main problem you need to solve is ____, is that right?
- If I could solve ____, would that give you what you need?
- What you are saying is that ____ is the number one thing you need solved?

Gaining Leverage to Close the Sale

Leverage to close questions can sometimes be harder to get answered because some people are reluctant to tell you their innermost reasons for to what they want. Sometimes they don't even know themselves. You really have to probe and listen carefully.

Craig was able to listen closely and uncover that Phillip, the IT systems buyer, wanted stress reduction in his life so he could disconnect from work and enjoy more leisure time. Tracy had to uncover that her prospect wanted more than an investment tool. She focused on the leverage gained when it was revealed that her prospect ultimately desired certainty that they would have their retirement getaway even if they underestimated future savings.

When you get the prospect to admit the big end game result they really want, and you can deliver that result, you are practically guaranteed a sale if your presentation was with a qualified prospect.

Sample Leverage Questions

- What would it mean to you if ____ (the main need) was fulfilled?
- By my delivering what I promised, how do you see yourself benefiting?

- How will my coming through for you help you reach your goals?
- What is the big end-game result you want?
- How do you see yourself personally benefiting by us working together?
- How do you see yourself using the $100,000 minimum ROI we guarantee?
- How do you envision your business growing by us working together?
- What will an X% growth in your department mean for you?
- Where does an X% return on the investment fit into your overall goals strategy?
- What is the main satisfaction or objective I can fulfill for you?

Avoiding F.U.E.L. Clogs

When people find that F.U.E.L. is not accelerating their closing percentages, it is usually because:

#1 They are asking questions that can be answered with a yes or no response. The rep is asking questions that set the prospect up to give a brief answer.

To ignite your sales F.U.E.L., your questions *must be* open-ended. If you ask a question that the prospect can answer by saying yes or no, then the prospect is not opening up. Your questions are actually doing the reverse of what is intended. You are shutting down the conversation.

A question such as, "Is that your wife in that picture?" can be answered with yes or no which gives you minimal information.

If you catch yourself falling into the trap of asking a yes or no question, follow up with a question that requires a more detailed answer such as "How did you meet her" or "tell me about where that photo was taken." However, this requires you to ask many more questions and that can irritate some of your prospects, especially those that are more defensive or guarded with sales people.

#2 **They have lost control of the presentation.**

Stay in control of the presentation. If the prospect takes control the presentation it is likely to stall.

Whoever is asking the questions is in control. If the prospect starts the presentation by asking you all the questions they are in control.

You need to ask questions to learn about their needs before they start asking you questions. That is a MUST, otherwise you do not have the insights of how to discuss key points in a way that supports their main objectives.

> **PRO TIP:** If a prospect won't answer questions that help you understand their needs then it's usually not worth doing the sales presentation.

If you're being rushed to present facts and features about your service before asking questions that at a minimum uncover needs, say "I need to know my clients so I can serve them effectively. If I can't ask you a few questions, I won't be able to do that."

Avoid this challenge altogether by taking control within the first minute or two of the presentation.

After an initial pleasantry or two, subtly take control by saying, "To save time and to focus specifically on your situation, can I ask you a few questions?"

Another favorite many of the people we have trained use is, "We tailor all our offerings to each customer's ____, ____, and ____. To save time and tailor things to your needs can I ask a few questions?"

Then *assume the YES* and start asking a few questions. No need to wait for a formal reply. A simple pause will do just fine.

Those "bridges" to your asking questions work perfectly because everyone wants to save time and loves things tailored to them because they all think their situation is unique.

It also allows you to set the tone of the focus being on them and cutting out a bunch of general info that is not relevant to them. It works like a charm every time.

#3 They are forgetting to make the prospect admit and feel their pain.

More of your sales success will be based on what the prospect says rather than what you say. Keep them talking. The more they open up and share what is missing from their current situation the more likely they are to buy from you. The more the prospect does the talking, especially at the start of the presentation, the more likely they are to buy. Their talking more equals a higher closing percentage. You talk more, especially early on, and you will have a lower closing percentage.

#4 Lastly, the biggest sales presentation sin related to F.U.E.L. is not using it.

Reps who are over-confident in their presentation and understanding of the prospect's needs go right into talking about what they have to offer. This prevents the prospect from clearly tuning into the reason why both parties are meeting, which is to solve the prospect's problem.

I Crashed and Burned Without F.U.E.L.

Sometimes losing a sale or two can make you a fortune if you are willing to learn from the experience.

PILLAR 3: Sales

No matter how great a sales superstar you think you are, you need to take control of the presentation early, and uncover the prospect's needs. Even if you are positive you know exactly what they need, you must get them to admit it. If you skip this step, your potential to close drops drastically which seriously hinders your 7 Figure progress.

Early in my career I crashed and burned while making an advertising sales presentation to an Army Colonel.

When I had my college sports magazine publishing business, some of our best prospects were military recruiting offices. I would meet with the ranking officer and get them to tell me how great their college scholarship opportunities were, how their programs would give college students financial relief, leadership experience, unmatched training, and numerous other benefits.

For many students, exploring a few years of military service in return for all the benefits offered could be a perfect fit and great solution.

After getting the recruiting officers to share all the benefits they offered, I asked them to *explain* the challenges that prevented them from telling more students about what they offered. I asked them to *share* with me the *problems* they faced getting on campus and in front of students, even though the military recruiters were offering them many great tuition reimbursement options.

The recruiters were proud of their message and their offers, and were excited to promote them. But every time I asked the recruiters to explain or share their frustrations about the things that blocked them from getting their message out, they immediately felt the need for a solution. My solution.

However, getting all this information made each presentation take extra time.

When one recruiter after another gave me very similar answers I was 100% positive about what they offered and what they needed. Then one day I met with an Army Colonel.

As soon as I walked in he was stern and direct. "Thank you young man for being prompt. Let's get down to business. Tell me what you've got." I told him how I needed to ask him a few questions to save time and understand his needs. His reply, "You have five minutes."

I said, "Okay, here is the problem you have and here is what we are going to do to fix it." Then a 20-something-year-old kid proceeded to tell a 50-something-year-old Colonel about his problems and the solution he needed. He responded with, "Thank you, I will take it under advisement."

I followed up but he never took my call again. Oh well, you can't get them all, I thought. I had so many other recruiting offices to reach across the country it was no big deal.

My biggest issue was time. Now that I knew the recruiters needs and what they wanted I started to cut some corners on my presentation.

I met with other recruiting officers and promptly told them about their problems reaching college students and how my publications and billboards would solve their challenges. Interestingly, most of these officers also told me, "Thank you, I'll take it under consideration." I quickly learned this was military-speak for No Sale.

Hmm. Each time I did the long version of the presentation where they shared all the benefits they offered as well as their pain related to getting the message out, they had a totally different reply. "Excellent, we will take this right up the chain of command." That turned out to be military-speak for, "We want it."

As soon as I went back to the long version of the presentation, the one where they always shared their problems early and they did most of the speaking at the start of our meeting, the sales rolled in.

LESSON LEARNED!

Make sure you get the prospect to admit their needs to both you and themselves.

I may have crashed and burned with a few of those officers early on but the lesson learned did more for improving my closing percentage than anything else. You must make sure the foundation of your sales process is based on getting your prospect to give you a long answer related to their pains and what they need from you to fix it.

F.U.E.L. Checklist

☐ Use it to learn rather than sell
☐ Uncover needs before presenting facts and features
☐ Dig deep, far below surface needs to increase closing percentages
☐ Get the prospect's why without settling for generalizations
☐ Gain leverage, have the prospect clearly define the result desired
☐ Relax and be yourself
☐ Consistently use it

F.U.E.L. is not used to "sell your product."

Notice in each of the examples in this section the reps were *not* selling — they were finding out what their prospects were looking for.

You MUST learn the needs of your prospect before you can position your product to solve them.

If you use sales F.U.E.L. and do what Craig, Tracy and countless other reps have done you will be exceptionally effective. Most salespeople don't dig deep enough into the prospect's specific needs to find out what it means to have those needs satisfied.

A salesperson makes a sale when they go beyond a prospect's general statements of "I want more business," "I want to make more money," or "I want XYZ to improve." You must find out what the prospect really wants on a deeper level.

> **PRO TIP:** Remember prospects definitely don't want a quote or a widget. They want the result the purchase gives them.

It is essential to get the real why, to get an answer that has specifics to it. Have them really open up. Ask them to explain what they mean when they answer your questions with vague generalizations. If they answer your questions with a broad generalization such as more business, higher sales, a better rate of return or more energy, don't except it. Instead, follow up and ask them to DEFINE what they mean. Have them expand on their answer.

Remember to relax. Just talk to your prospect and don't be afraid to ask questions.

Genuine connection and conversation is your greatest sales tool. Recognize you have the natural ability to use the most effective sales tools ever: Ask open-ended questions and listen to the answers.

Consistently utilize F.U.E.L. effectively to increase your closing ratio and to Join The 7-Figure Club.

Creating Your Own F.U.E.L. Blend

You need to tailor questions to your product or service. Observe what others have done. Borrow from them, copy them and then tweak and adjust based on what is right for your situation.

Open-ended questions work for each and every industry

F.U.E.L. is a structured way to plan out the questions you will ask prospects.

As we have emphasized, the heart of the technique is to ask questions that uncover the prospect's needs and difficulties.

Below are questions successfully utilized by the sales teams of 7 Figure Club members.

The industries are varied but the structure of the questions is similar. Many of their questions will be appropriate for your presentations.

Utilize their questions, modify where needed, and *most importantly write down five or six questions* you can use with your prospects.

> **PRO TIP:** Asking powerful sales questions that get the prospect to reveal their buying motivation must not be left to chance. Systemize your questions. Make your best presentations repeatable by making sure each presentation starts on the foundation of asking good questions right from the start, each and every time!

Uncovering Needs for Moving & Storage Companies

Friendly Vibe Questions
- Tell me a bit about what made you decide to move?
- What are some of the things you like about the school system and community you are moving to?
- That piece is clearly an antique, could you tell me a bit about it?
- Moving to a new location is exciting, which aspects of it are you most excited about?

Uncovering Needs Questions
- Which aspects concern you the most about the moving process?
- Please explain what you liked and didn't like about your experiences with other firms?
- Tell me what can we do to make you feel more comfortable and less stressed during this process?
- Tell me about the specific items that need special attention, and where you would want me to direct my men to take extra special care?
- How can we help make the moving process much easier for you?
- What are the top 3 things required to ensure that you are 100% satisfied?

Uncovering Needs for Contractors
- What is taking place in the home that made you call about ____?
- Tell me a bit about the last time you had contracting work done

- What are your main concerns related to the installation?
- Share a bit about you what frustrates you about your (kitchen, bath, yard, etc.)
- Can you explain your top 3 objectives?
- What issue motivated you to want to change ____?

Uncovering Needs for Office Equipment Dealers

- What is lacking with your current solution?
- How will you be judging improved performance?
- Share a bit about your current solution, what works and what needs improving?
- What challenges are you tasked with solving?
- What problems are being caused by the gap you mentioned?
- How is this difficulty preventing you from hitting your targets, objectives, etc?

How to Handle Objections

Create standard responses for your most common objections.

Every presentation is bound to have an objection or two. Objections are a normal part of the sales process and should be expected.

No matter how perfect your presentation and how well-suited your product is for a highly qualified prospect, everyone faces objections. Top producers structure their presentations in a way that handles objections before they even become a major factor, and also have their preferred ways to overcome objections. They also have a different mindset about objections.

The following tips will help you better understand how they view those situations.

Objections can be one of the most frustrating parts of the sales process but with proper preparation that can be minimized, so don't let it get you flustered. Keep the following rules in mind when any objection comes up and you'll be able to deal with them easily.

If you seem to get the same objections frequently, it's best to know exactly what to say before going into the sales presentation. You can have your best rebuttals to common objections prepared so that you can easily move past the objection and on to the closing portion of your presentation. EVEN MORE IMPORTANTLY, top producers recognize that if they get an objection frequently then they work on addressing it as part of the presentation.

12 Ways Superstars View Overcoming Objections

1. *Ideally address any objections BEFORE the prospect can even state them as an objection.*

    Try to get the prospect's reason for not buying out in the open quickly. If you get the sense that the prospect is hesitating on buying, ask them what the reason is. Get the objection handled early and quickly so you can move on to the next stage of your presentation. By addressing the objection while casually chatting rather than when you are asking for a buying commitment you minimize some of its power.

    When you address their issue before asking for the order you are simply answering a question or addressing a concern. When stated at the close, their issue has grown into their reason to not buy, their reason to say no, all of which have much more psychological weight.

2. *Keep yourself in a confident mental state.*

    Maintain a mindset where you know you are delivering quality and value. Then ask for the order. Believe and recognize your prospect is ready, willing and able to pay for that value.

    When you have a confident attitude about the value you deliver, your ability to persuade the prospect to buy your product becomes much more effective.

3. *It's your job to minimize any objections the prospect might have, and you can do that by being as informative as possible.*

    Often, when the prospect has objections, it's because they don't have enough evidence to believe that the value you offer is factual. Don't let this happen.

> **PRO TIP:** Top producers see objections as a request for more information and reframe the objection as the prospect pointing out that they didn't cover something well enough for their prospect to be ready to buy. This is a very different attitude than thinking they are potentially being rejected.

4. *Don't argue with the prospect.*

    This should be obvious. Arguing with a prospect isn't going to get you anywhere.

    You may prove yourself right and "win" the argument, but show the prospect that they are wrong and you'll most definitely lose the sale.

5. *Rephrase the prospect's objection in your own words before responding to it.*

    If the objection is worth responding to, you should restate it to them to show that you're listening.

    Prospects want to know you have heard them and understood them. This makes them comfortable, aligns each of you and thus brings you closer to the sale.

6. *Agree with the prospect on a point related to their objection before responding.*

    This helps to cushion your answer so it doesn't seem as though you're seeing their objection as invalid.

    For example, tell them how you can understand how they could feel that way in order to form a point of agreement. Agreement aligns you with your prospect rather than taking opposite sides which can subconsciously be confrontational. Also ask them why they feel the way they do, or their process for forming the objection.

7. *Whenever someone states something is expensive it is especially helpful to learn how they formed that opinion.*

    If they think something is expensive top producers will confidently ask a prospect, "expensive compared to what?"

    Once they understand the prospect's logic, a top producer can go into the reasons why the prospect doesn't need to worry about that particular objection.

    When countering a prospect's reasons, out of reflex it is tempting to say "but" before going into the objection counter — don't do that. When you say that word, all the prospect will hear is that you disagree with them, regardless of whether or not you agreed with them about anything before.

8. *Don't react negatively to the prospect's objection.*

    While clearly trivial objections can and should be ignored, if you can tell that the prospect is truly concerned about a particular objection, always treat it with respect.

9. *Keep your responses brief.*

    While we want to treat objections with respect, regardless of whether or not they are trivial, when you do respond, don't give the objection so much weight that you overly validate the objection. Make your point in as few words as possible.

10. *Don't dwell on the objection.*

If you respond to the objection and the prospect seems as though they want to dispute your response, make sure you have adequately substantiated your reasoning. On the other hand, don't debate them. You and the prospect can disagree on an issue but still move forward with the sale if enough value has been created. As mentioned previously, arguing with a prospect will get you nowhere,

11. *Be confident in your response to the objection and lead the prospect back to saying, "yes."*

Once you have responded to an objection, don't ask if that response was sufficient. Immediately go on with the sales talk. As you transition back to your presentation or close, get the prospect to give you a small "Yes." I.e. ask, "Does that make sense" or "Do you understand the reason for X now," etc. We want to get the prospect comfortable saying yes to us. Shift them off of the negative and onto saying yes to you even if it is on a small point such as understanding your explanation.

12. *Don't make up a response to an objection.*

It's better to admit you're not sure about a point and would need to get answers to the objection/issue, rather than getting something wrong in your explanation.

Last and most importantly, **ask "WHY?"** to answer objections. This is a powerful little word. *Why* is the *most important word* you can use when overcoming objections.

When someone states their objection, ask why they think that. It keeps the prospect talking and can often give you additional perspective on the prospect's views which will enable you to form a better response.

> **PRO TIP:** One of my favorite ways to use "why" is when someone says the price is too high. When I respond with "Why do you say that" or "Compared to what" (in order to learn why) the objection often loses credibility. It allows you to see how they are viewing the issue and then you can easily re-establish value.

High Price: An Objection or a Benefit?

One of our contracting clients was by far the most expensive in his area. He was always the highest bid. Of course that generated an objection, so we created a standard response for it.

During our sales training program, his team learned to state early in the presentation, "I will most likely be your highest quote, and it is because we do ___, ___, and ___." Then his team went on to explain several guarantees they offered that solved several common problems prospects had. They emphasized how those problems will not be an issue, and they list why that was the case. Each rep then confidently stated how with his firm you get the best, and that is why the cost is higher.

Countless condo boards and property managers then felt happy to buy "the best."

The contractor observed that his high price point was his most common objection and the biggest challenge his team had to overcome. Once they started to directly address the higher price objection as part of the sales presentation instead of waiting till the prospect brought it up, we were able to turn it into a benefit of hiring his firm instead of an obstacle.

> **PRO TIP:** By learning the best way to present your product and how to reframe what an objection can mean you can minimize many issues. In many cases you can even turn objections info evidence of your value and a reason to buy.

Closing: The easiest part of the presentation

Many people think closing is the hardest part of the sales presentation. It is actually the easiest.

However, 6 specific steps must be followed for that to be the case:

1. *You must have a qualified prospect.* It is impossible to close an unqualified prospect. To have a qualified prospect you must a) speak with the actual decision maker that has b) the need for your services and c) the money to pay for the value you offer. When all three pieces are in place there is an excellent chance you can close the deal. Anything less than having all three of those pieces and your odds of closing drop dramatically.
2. *Understand the value and benefits your decision maker desires.* Once you have *directly asked* your prospect to define what is most important and uncovered what they need you have the green light to move forward with your presentation
3. *Realize what really motivates them.* Once you understand your prospect's true motivations, a clear and direct discussion that explains how your product or service satisfies their needs connects all the dots. You are showing them how you deliver the solution required at the value they desire.

4. *Test for their opinion.* Now that everything has been lined up, test if they are ready to move forward. Ask "in your opinion how does everything look/feel/sound to you?" People don't always like to make decisions but they love to share their opinion. If they give you positive feedback move forward. If you sense some resistance then present more evidence, build more value, or uncover a greater need.
5. *Make buying their idea.* People love to buy and resist being sold. If they can satisfy their needs and have found a great value, they love to buy. If the evidence and information presented supports them getting what they want at the price they can afford then buying is the obvious next step.
6. *Make buying easy. Simply ask them to buy.* You don't need a bunch of fancy closes, strategies or techniques. When they told you they like what they heard ask them to take the next step forward. Invite them to buy.

Each of those steps are the natural progression of a qualified prospect moving forward. Recognize them. When each is in place they are waving you in. They are ready to buy. Now ask them to take the next required action to wrap up the order.

Some easy ways to ask for the order are:
- Let's get started, okay?
- Would you prefer ____ or ____?
- I will get you scheduled for next week.
- Which credit card will you be using?

Be proud that you have presented the solution that helped someone satisfy their needs and delivered a good value. Every time you do that you should hold your head up high, ask for the order, and close confidently.

Double or Triple Your Closing Percentage

Sales and closing really are pretty simple.

You find and call on an abundance of qualified prospects. During your presentation, you learn that your product or service is a great fit as you take them through each of the six phases of prepping to close.

But the reality is sometimes prospects get scared. Some are fearful of making a decision, others are not decisive, or genuinely need to receive a call back.

Although you should ask for the order multiple times in those situations, in the real world many prospects will require a call back. Many products actually require a multiple-step close for a variety of reasons.

To double or triple your firms closing percentage the biggest obstacle standing in your way is not budget, product availability or any of the other justifications/excuses reps give.

Reps fail to close because they fail to adequately follow up on their leads.

Many reps do not follow up on a lead enough times to actually get a busy prospect into the sales funnel.

Other reps are sure they can read the prospect's mind and therefore can predict with absolute certainty who will buy after their presentation. Mistakenly, they only follow up with red-hot opportunities. It's laughable.

Improve lead follow-up in every stage of your sales process and your team's closing percentage will jump off the charts.

Follow-up is something that sets top producers apart from average producers. It helps the best producers become superstars.

A few Shocking Follow-up Numbers

48% of reps NEVER follow up
25% of reps stop after TWO follow ups
12% will only try 3 times
12% (1 in 8) of reps will follow up 4 or MORE times

Why Follow-up Is Essential

A mere 2% of leads close on the first call
3% close on the second call
5% on the 3rd call
10% close on the 4th call
80% of leads close somewhere between the 5th and 12th contact or contact attempt (you may not reach them every time you try, but those still count in the closing process).

Please don't give yourself a NO SALE. *Follow up. Make the prospect decide.*

Some additional closing leverage

Text your prospect some extra info (that's relevant) during your call and the close rate goes up by as much as 40%

I.e. "Hey, I wanted to send you a case study," article, rendering, SOMETHING. You get their cell number and set yourself apart from other reps.

Triple leverage

1. Send them 3 texts and the close rate triples. (The texts must be spaced apart over time, not 3 texts sent all at once.)

PILLAR 3: Sales

2. Write each day's numbers down. ("Numbers" means calls, presentations, follow-ups, results.) This will give you weekly and monthly totals.

3. Tracking written, accurate numbers is essential. Those numbers become your baseline for performance. When you grow your team, your baseline performance numbers will guarantee you are not snowed, misled, etcetera by any of your staff since you know what call volume and appointment volume yields a sale.

Now go set some new records and leave your competition in your dust!

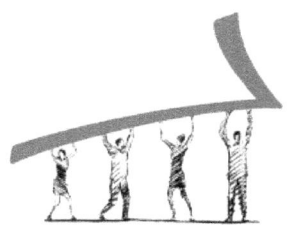

PILLAR 4
MARKETING — SCALING YOUR SALES

Marketing & Sales Success Formula:
Strong Flow of Quality Leads = Strong Sales
Weak Flow of Leads = Weak Sales & Limited Growth

Without sales, you don't have a business, and without leads you don't have sales. I've always thought of sales and marketing as the right and left arm of the business. You need both, and they complement each other. To really scale your business, you need lots of leads. Leads are a function of your marketing department. A steady and strong flow of quality leads pouring into the business is exactly what the sales team needs.

It's that simple. Don't overcomplicate it.

Build a Marketing Tool Box

To get an abundance of leads flowing into the sales department, there are numerous options. The type of business you have, along with the growth stage your business is currently in, will influence which tools will make the most sense to use. We are going to cover **TEN** options. I call them channels. Think of each channel as one of the tools in your marketing toolbox. And most of these tools could be used by almost any business.

It is shocking how few businesses expand on the options in their marketing toolbox. They find one or two ways to generate leads, and then they stop. Hey, I'm all for having a few favorite methods that are tried and proven, but when you have more marketing channels, you open up more lead options. More marketing channels means more leads.

Testing a variety of channels also means you may find a gold mine of new opportunity. *Test*, *test*, and *keep* testing.

Are Your Marketing Efforts Profitable?

As you test ways to get more out of each of your favorite marketing channels and explore new channels, you must ALWAYS keep **ROAS** in mind.

ROAS stands for **R**eturn **O**n **A**d **S**pend. Even when you are not actually buying ads, you need to be looking at your return on marketing dollars spent. What is the number of leads generated from each marketing campaign? What was the cost of each lead generated? What was the marketing cost for each sale that was made? What percentage of each sale went to marketing costs?

You must know these numbers. Chart your ROAS and other key marketing stats.

A major mistake growing businesses make is failing to spend enough on marketing. Then when they do spend more on marketing, they fail to direct the dollars toward what is working and OVERSPEND on the marketing that is not working. You need to know the ROI (Return on Investment) of each of your marketing initiatives.

The ROAS Formula

1. Know your ad spend. Add up all the expenses for running your ad
2. Know the number of sales you received from the lead source
3. Divide the ad spend amount by number of leads to get your cost per lead

    I.e. SPEND $1000 on an ad and you received 10 leads $1000 divided by 10 = $100 per lead

    Don't stop there. Knowing your cost per lead is critical but we are looking for return on our advertising investment or ROAS.
4. How many sales came from those 10 leads and what was the total value of those sales?

Did your 10 leads generate $9000 in sales, $20,000, or $2000?

You need to know this to calculate your Return on the Ad Spend (ROAS).

Let's plug in the numbers to learn your Return On Ad Spend.

Sales divided by cost of advertising gives you the return.

If you got $9000 in sales and spent $1000 the return was 9 to 1 (9K divided by 1K = 9).

Also realize that 11% of each sale went to an advertising expense.

If you made 20k in sales your return was 20 to 1 (20K divided by 1K = 20).

That means only 5% of each sale went to an ad expense.

But in our third example our $1000 in advertising yielded only $2000 in sales. Therefore, 2000 divided by 1000 = 2, so for each ad dollar spent you received 2 dollars in sales. **CAUTION**: This does not mean you doubled your money. You have other expenses such as costs on goods sold.

> **PRO TIP:** WATCH OUT for all the advertising and marketing people that will tell you "CONGRATULATIONS" we just doubled your money.

The number is fairly meaningless without knowing your other costs.

In this case, we did get a two to 1 return on our ad spend BUT Advertising was 50% of the sale.

Therefore this may or may not be a profitable sale.

Cupcakes: Hobby, Side Hustle or Viable Business?

I was working with a baker, a lovely woman that took such pride in her cupcakes. Everyone told her how great they were, and she tested whether people would buy them by promoting them at the local market each Sunday.

Everyone raved about them. They looked gorgeous and when kids walked past her cupcake display, the eye appeal had each child pulling the parents toward her bake stand. Adults would see them and instantly knew they would be perfect for gifts or for a well-deserved treat. She was so happy with her sales and the response she was getting.

Her concept was being validated. Her ego and self-worth were soaring. She was sure she had a thriving business. She was selling $750 to $1000 in cupcakes each Sunday afternoon on average. She beamed with pride as she told me

PILLAR 4: Marketing

her sales numbers. I gave her a look that said "think about that for a second." She smiled and said, "Oh that's right. I had to pay $250 each week for the spot at the market." (That was her marketing cost.)

She adjusted her calculations and said she was making $500 to $750 each weekend. Not a 7 Figure Club business, but the beginning of a nice little side hustle. She was still very happy.

In her case what was her ROAS or ROI on marketing spend?

On a $1000 day she was getting a 4 to 1 return on her investment of $250 for her fee to sell at the Sunday market. Said another way, 25% of each sale went to her booth/marketing cost.

On her $750 days, she was getting a 3 to 1 return and 33% of each day's take went to her marketing cost (space rental in this instance).

She still believed she was making between $500 and $700 minus "a little for ingredients." After all flour, sugar, water and the other ingredients were not *that* expensive.

It was an error so many business owners make, and one that will kill profitability long before an entrepreneur can get near the 7 Figure Club entrance. Whether it is a new business working toward their first 50K or someone doing 500K, you must know all your costs. This allows you to make decisions like a leader, like the CEO you are.

You see, *thinking* your ingredient expenses are low, versus *factually knowing* what those expenses are, are two different things.

When we had her look at exact costs receipt by receipt for ingredients it turned out she was paying about $250 each weekend for ingredients.

When we totaled the $250 for space plus the $250 for ingredients the cost number suddenly climbed to $500 each weekend. Her take was now $250 to $500 in profit. She was still happy with her side hustle, but she also immediately started to see things more clearly.

By knowing her total costs, she started to look at her growing business differently. She started taking into account rainy days, spoilage, the cost of gas and even her own time. She started thinking about what the marketing and other costs needed to be in order to have money for an assistant, all while remaining profitable.

When you know what percentage of each sale is going to marketing, you have an essential building block in calculating profitability. When you combine marketing costs with cost of goods sold, you see if the lead-channel being examined makes sense to scale and grow. As always, you must also calculate your other expenses such as payroll, taxes, and more.

From the moment you acquire a lead and start gaining sales traction you *must know* what percentage of sales goes to marketing costs, and then add that to your cost of goods sold. Is there enough left to have your marketing channel be viable?

How Much Can You Spend on Ads?

Some businesses have huge margins. The bigger the margin, the more you can spend on advertising to generate leads and thereby fuel sales. Other businesses have really tight margins. I'm so envious of my friends who sell digital products online versus my ecommerce business (**BulkOfficeSupply.com**) where we sell office and cleaning supplies at super thin margins. We sell those items at a huge discount which is wonderful for our customers, and those low prices are one of our competitive advantages, but it can make marketing harder. It required me to develop the practice of becoming very selective about marketing choices in order to grow sales to well over 8 figures.

Let me share a lesson about how knowing my numbers helped me make marketing decisions.

It helped me avoid marketing sales reps who were selling digital tools that would have generated sales where we lost money. Every marketing rep or advertising rep makes their tools sound great. Each shows you examples of how they helped another firm make sales. When we review our marketing (and potential new tools) we must know if the sales being generated are sales that are profitable, and that grow the business profitably.

Because we sold office and cleaning supplies at razor thin margins, we had a very high cost of goods sold. In many cases it was 75%. That means when we make a $100 sale $75 comes right off the top to pay suppliers. That leaves only 25% gross profit and we still had other expenses that needed to be covered such as rent, payroll, and credit card fees before we got to the holy grail of net profit. This shows us that in most cases we would need to keep advertising costs to somewhere between 3% and 5%.

We received calls and emails from ad reps daily. Frequently they would boast how based on their analysis of our website they were sure we would get a 3 to 1 return, and at a minimum double our money. Because I knew my numbers, I knew this was bad. We needed a 20 to 1 return in order to have ad spend remain in the 5% of total sales range.

Scaling with Tight Margins

Finding marketing tools that yield $20 in sales for each $1 spend is hard. In many cases it is rare. Knowing your numbers really is your best friend in navigating the fine line between marketing opportunity and risk. Finding a 20 to 1 ROAS was a challenge. In order to scale we selectively made ad purchases that could be as high as 25% of the sales generated, or a 4 to 1 ROAS.

How is that possible when the actual hard good cost was often 75% and we still had other expenses to cover?

The answer is based on building customers rather than making an individual sale.

What is the Lifetime Value (LTV) of your customer?

How often will they return and be a repeat customer?

A sale might only be $100, but if the customer returns monthly then you have generated $1000 or more per year. If that customer returns year after year then the number is significantly higher. You must track the numbers so you know the facts. You must cultivate the customer relationship. You are not in business to make a one-time sale. You are in business to build a loyal following.

Once you know the *lifetime value*, aka the *repeat value*, of a customer you can consider acquiring customers at breakeven or even a slight loss. The Repeat Factor aka the Return Factor can have some marketing channels with a low ROAS actually perform very well when basing return on a *predictable* lifetime, or recurring revenue model.

For instance, a martial arts school or a dance school charges $1500 for a 6-month package. After calculating costs, they decided they can spend as much as $500 to acquire a new student and still break even. They also know that at a minimum 50% of their students will renew for another 3 to 6 months, and many others will continue for even longer. In addition to that, they know that new students also bring in friends and family (aka referrals). Therefore even if an ad channel cost them $750 to acquire a new customer, they would be still be okay once we factor in that the average customer actually brings in much more than $1500. In their case closer to a $2250 minimum, plus referrals.

If a business proactively plans how to keep in touch with their customers, and continually delivers a quality experience they will significantly increase the lifetime value of each of their customers. Build a business that is focused on relationships and repeat business rather than on transactions.

Every business can develop a lifetime customer value strategy. Notice a few of the strategies some of our coaching clients utilized. Each was easy to do, very affordable, and paid huge dividends. What approach can you add in as a formal marketing process?

For example: If a realtor cultivates their relationships, they can do much more than one transaction with an individual. If an auto center does good honest work and delivers excellent customer service, the first sale will lead to many others. If a new customer has a great experience in a local restaurant they will likely be back, especially if the owner develops a reminder campaign. E-commerce stores can email their customers new offers, specials and new product announcements. Medical offices can remind their patients to come in for checkups. A bakery can let past customers know they can preorder to be guaranteed their favorite treats, plus have it ready and waiting so they bypass the holiday lines. Remember, sometimes getting more business from a past customer can be as basic as having a consistent process where you follow up with a phone call, text, or email to say, "Thank You."

KNOWING the numbers will allow you to prudently scale, and build a foundation on which to grow your 7 Figure Club business.

5 Marketing Mistakes that Kill Sales

Sales Killer #1: Not Testing

Numerous variables effect which ad copy, sources of media, and sales approaches will influence your prospects. Guessing or having the ego to "know" what will motivate the marketplace to buy is a sure way to kill opportunity.
- You must test your offers.
- You must test your copy.
- You must test the medium used.
- You must test position of ad in the medium used.
- You must test timing of your ads and offers.

YOU MUST TEST EVERYTHING

Simply Put:
> TEST
> TEST
> TEST

I was working with a client with a business that sold janitorial products. They wanted to give a purchase incentive and decided to offer their prospects a $25 gift card to either Starbucks or Old Navy. The owners personally always liked a good discount and putting a bit of extra money in their pocket, so they thought an offer which would directly benefit the office managers they were targeting would be the way to go.

We brought up the idea of a 10% discount on the order's cost instead of the gift cards, but they believed it wouldn't pull as well. Why would they prefer a discount on cleaning supplies more than getting their coffee free for a week they asked? My response was that we really don't know. I recommended that we do a 50/50 split test.

The offer for the 10% discount outperformed the gift card 7 to 1. Although the owners of the janitorial supply firm personally preferred something going in their pocket, their prospects, the office managers, chose the discount by a landslide.

TEST, TEST, and TEST, rather making decisions based on your own biases.

___

___

___

Sales Killer #2: Advertising for Recognition rather than Results

So much advertising is recognition-driven. Some marketing "gurus" even call it branding. Advertising that promotes the company name, number of years in business, vague claims, and an ego-serving list of facts is rarely cost effective for small business owners. Billboards, banners, premium incentive items and many print ads often lack a specific way to track results.

You are advertising for results. *Run ads that offer clear benefits to your prospect and get them to take at least one step into the sales pipeline.*

Get something from your ad that builds relationship, credibility and your database:
- Your ad can offer a free report.
- Your ad can offer a free consultation.
- Your ad can directly ask the prospect to call.
- Your ad can directly ask for the sale (small offer a good 1st step).

Ads that get results ask for something trackable. Give them a reason to take action.

By tracking ad performance, you can calculate your return on ad spend (ROAS), lead cost, and cost of sales. This allows you to invest in advertising rather than speculate on it.

> **PRO TIP:** What can you give your customer that makes them want to give you their contact information?

_____

_____

_____

Sales Killer #3: Not Having or Not Knowing Your *Unique Selling Proposition*

Most businesses ineffectively attempt to distinguish themselves from the competition because they use the same statements as the competition.

For instance, when working with restaurant owners I ask most of the owners to tell me what makes them unique.

PILLAR 4: Marketing

Ninety percent respond by saying something along the lines of "We serve quality food, provide good service in a nice atmosphere, and all at a fair price."

Aren't those things a given?

They are hardly unique.

You need to understand what makes you *unique*, and then promote that. That is your Unique Selling Proposition ("U.S.P.")

Is your chef from the CIA, the Culinary Institute of America? Are your burgers the biggest in town? Do you brew your beer on premises? Do you have the largest selection of California wines in the area? Do you grow your own vegetables? Are your ingredients locally sourced? Find something to say that the competition isn't saying. Or start *saying* something that no one else is saying, even if everyone does it.

I saw an ad for an oil change service. They promoted that every oil change came with a 69-point safety inspection. Sounds impressive and no other competitor offered it. All they did was check the tire pressure, all the other fluids, wiper blades, etc. Every quick-lube place and dealership does that. They just stated it in a way that gave them a competitive advantage.

What makes you unique?

What do you offer that is special?

What can you do, say or offer, that is DIFFERENT?

You must develop your U.S.P.!

Three highly competitive industries are overnight delivery services, pizza and car rentals.

We all know the U.S.P. of FedEx, Dominos and Avis. "When it absolutely, positively needs to be there," "Hot, fresh and fast," and "We try harder" were all U.S.P.s that had them take market share from the competition.

How will the market place know you?

_____

_____

_____

Sales Killer #4: No Residual or Add on Sale

Most people focus on the value of the first sale rather than the lifetime value of the customer. This causes them to lose many sales opportunities from each customer and/or prospect in their database.

- Statistically, how often does your average customer buy?

_____

- What is the industry's average? Are you above or below that average?

_____

- What additional services does your customer need?

_____

- What businesses would be an appropriate "strategic partner?"

_____

- How could you be compensated for referring businesses to your strategic partners?

_____

PILLAR 4: Marketing

- Are you marketing to your prospects and non-buyers?

_____

- Who else would find your database valuable?

_____

You can often make more profit from the add-on sale than you can from the main product, or initial sale.

You must find ways to turn that first sale into more revenues. Each of the add-on sales will significantly increase profits.

Notice what each of the big players does:

Go to a fast food restaurant and they ask you if you want to make it a large. That extra soda and some additional fries are filled with more profit than calories. You rent a car, and they sell you insurance, the convenience of a prepaid gas tank, and of course the upgrade. Restaurants can double the size of the check with cocktails, appetizers, and desserts thus turning a marginal table into a highly profitable one. What about any online purchases and TV offers? You buy one item, and suddenly you are offered four more specials before you can complete the purchase. By the time they are done, a breakeven transaction has been turned into a highly profitable sale.

In addition to the upsell, continually work to resell your past customers and get value from your database. It is an easy source of additional profits and fewer businesses tap into it.

_____

_____

Sales Killer # 5: Not Fully Knowing Your Customer's Specific Needs

Most companies, salespeople and their marketing campaigns address the needs of their prospects and customers with broad stroke generalities. Treating each prospect as part of the crowd and ASSUMING you know their specific needs is the ideal formula for mediocrity.

- You must learn your prospect's motivations!
- You must learn how fulfilling their need will impact their life!
- You must learn how they define fulfilling their need!
- You must learn what they want
- You must learn their evidence procedures for knowing their need is completely met

_____

_____

_____

Accurately and clearly fulfill your client's needs. Ask them what they need, survey them and listen to them. When you uncover more of what they want and need you increase satisfaction while exponentially increasing sales. More importantly you exponentially increase profits as well.

TOP 10 MARKETING CHANNELS

One of my favorite marketing geniuses is a legend in the field named Jay Abraham. He taught me the concept of the Marketing Parthenon. The Parthenon is a famous Greek building that has survived for thousands of years. The roof on most buildings is supported by 4 main points.

The Parthenon roof was supported by many pillars. Even if one gave way the integrity of the roof was upheld by each of the other pillars.

Jay explained that you need numerous "Marketing Pillars" to sustain and support your business. If one pillar fails to support your marketing efforts, your business will remain strong because each of the other pillars will support it.

Many businesses rely on *one* key marketing pillar. If that marketing channel stops performing, the business will go into a nosedive. You may crash and burn before a new strategy can be implemented. You must have multiple marketing channels in place. They will not perform equally, but you still need to have a diversified approach to generate quality leads and increase sales.

> **PRO TIP:** Have *at least* 3 to 6 marketing channels operational and consistently producing.

Let's look at a few ways to build your marketing mix. How many are you currently using? Which ones are relevant for your business, and which of those could you implement?

Marketing does not need to cost a fortune. Many effective marketing pillars can be put in place with minimal financial risk. In many cases, the only investment is time. Many quality leads, along with a substantial amount of sales, can be generated with low-cost marketing initiatives. Of the 10 marketing channels listed, notice that many of them require minimal cash flow. Which marketing approaches can you add to your mix? Which team members would be responsible for their success and how will you track effectiveness?

CHANNEL 1: NETWORKING

Networking is one of the lowest-cost strategies to market and attract quality leads.

There are numerous ways to network and a variety of networking groups to choose from, many of which are free or very low cost. When looking for a networking group find one that matches both your interests and the interests of the audience that is most likely to be a qualified prospect. Remember, "everyone" is not your target prospect. To get the most out of networking events you want to attend functions that are a target rich environment — meaning full of qualified prospects.

Don't sell at networking events

Don't sell at the functions. Meet people and figure a time to connect later. The goal is to get leads and plant the seeds for developing a relationship. Selling on the spot is inappropriate. Instead, ask about their needs, learn about the person you are speaking with. Use that information to become more valuable to them.

Manage your time at networking events

Don't spend too much time with any one person. After you have made a connection, exchanged contact info and created a reason to touch base again, move on to the next person. This allows you to meet more people, and for them to do the same.

Game mindset

Do go to the networking event with a **game mindset**. For example, have two goals:

PILLAR 4: Marketing

1) To introduce yourself to a specific number of people. It could be 5, 15, or 30, it doesn't matter. Just have a goal.

2) Have a specific outcome in mind that is measurable. E.g. I'm going to attend the event and get two good leads/contacts from the event. Or maybe your goal is 5 or some higher number.

With these two objectives PRE-PLANNED, you can leave the event with defined measurable results as a sure-fire way to gauge your success. Did you introduce yourself, and meet the number of people you planned? YES or NO? Did you get the number of qualified leads you intended? YES or NO?

Be honest about your outcomes. If you hit both objectives, good job, you won "the game." Should you set higher targets next time or did you perform great? If you underperformed, know the reason why. What will you do next time to grow your lead generation efforts?

Act like you're the host

Do act like you are the host rather than a guest. As the host you approach each visitor warmly, you proactively greet them, you ask about them and focus on them. Do this and you will meet lots of people, and have a great time doing it.

I remember a property-and-casualty insurance rep we coached. Restaurants were a great prospect for him so he started to attend restaurant-owner-focused networking functions. Rather than being the "insurance guy" that everyone wants to avoid, we had him attend with a "host" mindset.

He invited several of his current restaurant clients to the meeting. Before attending another meeting, he reached out to restaurant owners he didn't even know and invited them to the meeting. Members of the group took notice. The new guy was bringing more prospective members than anyone else. The established restaurant-owner members wanted to know more about him, the guests who didn't know anyone at the meeting stuck close to him and welcomed the introductions he could make. He was truly a host. He stood out as a person that delivered value. He became someone the members sought out, rather than an insurance guy that had to chase prospects.

Find creative ways to have networking work for you. Better yet, keep it simple and be a person that shows up willing to deliver value.

> **PRO TIP:** Make sure you ask the people you meet about them and talk about them. This is a great way to qualify the prospect. Do they have a need for your product or services, are they likely to afford it, are they the decision maker or can they put you in touch with the decision maker? Can they introduce you to your target audience, thus being a good source of referrals?

Take notes

Take notes when you are networking. If you are meeting a lot of people, you will not be able to remember everything.

In between meeting various people, send a text to yourself with some of the key things you want to remember about those people. It allows you to reconnect more seamlessly later. You can reference the vacation they mentioned, ask about their children by name, mention a sports team, key business topic, or strategy that was very relevant. It also positions you to be a resource, and someone that is on top of details.

I've been to many events where someone mentions something I can help with. It can be a restaurant recommendation, following up on a fact check or making an introduction for them. When I'm the one calling back with this information they are always grateful, and impressed with my attention to detail. Both valuable ways to be remembered.

I'm not a fan of taking notes while with the people. It looks tacky. Of course, every rule has exceptions. Sometimes someone says something that is genius. So that I don't risk forgetting it, I tell them that I think their idea is fantastic and that I must remember what they shared. I look them in the eye as I write down their wisdom. Everyone is always flattered. That said, you are jotting down a key point not keeping your pen out to interview them.

> **PRO TIP:** Be the one that follows up. Maybe one in 100 people that take your card or contact info actually reach out. Set yourself apart by reaching out to nurture the relationship. Since we all get busy, the easiest way to make sure this happens is to enter a reminder into your phone or calendar. And reach out to deliver value, not to hit them up for a sales presentation.

Finding networking groups

There are so many different networking groups.

Rotary is the largest networking organization in the world. Typically, the meetings are attended by business people in the local community who have an affinity for improving the community. It is more about contribution and connection than lead generation, but it's filled with business leaders. Go with the mindset of contribution, and you will be strong. Other community groups are Knights of Columbus, Kiwanis Club, and Lions Club to name a few.

Among my favorite are groups specifically designed for business people to network. One of the most affordable, and always filled with business professionals looking to connect, is the local Chamber of Commerce. There are also groups that charge a membership fee to put people together to exchange leads. BNI, Business Network International, is a huge organization with multiple chapters in every major city. Le Tip is similar. And of course you always have the option to start your own networking group.

These groups meet weekly or monthly for 1 to 2 hours each time. The goal is to exchange leads. You are developing a team of people who are on the lookout for your qualified prospect and when they find one they tell you at the next meeting. Also, the groups are usually non-competitive, i.e. only one plumber, one dentist, one insurance guy, etc.

As with any group, you want the type of people you and they work with to be a good match. I've been to groups where it was filled with sales reps from unrelated industries, such as personal chefs, a vitamin salesperson and others who didn't match my target market at the time — and I've been to groups where it was a target rich environment.

> **PRO TIP:** Visit the group several times before joining to be sure it is a group of good lead-providers rather than merely a group of good people. Your time is a valuable commodity.

CHANNEL 2: Referrals — aka FREE LEADS

One of the best and often underutilized sources of new leads is referrals. I'm sure you have gotten numerous referrals over the years. Heck, you probably get several referrals every month.

We all love referrals, they are a source of high quality leads, where you have a high closing percentage. It is also so much more fun to call on a warm lead rather than a cold call. From a marketing perspective, you are acquiring a lead essentially for free.

Six, Seven and Eight Figure Referrals

A good referral can add to your income but a great referral can transform your business. A referral can be more than an individual lead. It can also be an introduction to a strategic partner that can provide an ongoing source of leads. In other cases it can be a dream client or provide entrée into a new marketplace.

Through a networking group I received an introduction to a gentleman that had founded a major negotiation training firm. That led to him hiring me to present his programs throughout the world. The referral led to international speaking gigs, relationships with Fortune 500 firms, an entire new set of training programs, and six figures in additional income.

One of my clients received a tremendous amount of new business from a trade association. The association had listed him as one of their preferred vendors. This endorsement brought him highly qualified leads on a regular basis. Best of all, the resistance to closing was very low due to the fact that his firm was recommended by the association.

I asked for his help in getting a meeting with the vendor selection committee and he came through. His referral led to me being selected as a preferred vendor as well. This allowed me to pick up over 100 new monthly clients and an additional 7 figures in revenue. Associations are a great source of referral business. Ironically, you may need a referral to break through the admittance barriers.

Referrals are earned. It is your excellent work, your commitment to your present clients and customers, that has someone endorse you.

A client that advised people in the insurance and financial sectors introduced me to one of his clients. They had a small firm that sold B2B products. I was brought in to help them change their marketing and sales processes.

Through the coaching process their business continued to grow. The shifts in the business were so significant that I was made a full partner in the firm. Never underestimate the power of referrals, the doors that can be opened and the value that can be created. Opportunity is all around you. Opportunity is what you make of it. In this case it was an eight figures referral.

Ask for Referrals

While presenting referral workshops or during one on one coaching sessions, I playfully scratch my head and say to my clients, "I don't get it. Referrals are a super good source of leads and a source of highly profitable new clients BUT you don't have a formal marketing plan in place to get more referrals. Instead, you just wait for them to randomly show up, or get offered to you out of the blue.

Then I ask, "Why do you wait instead of proactively asking for the referrals?"

The top answers are:
- I didn't think to ask my customers
- I forgot to ask them
- I'm so busy working on my other lead sources I left this one alone

Are you making the same mistakes and leaving lots of sales and money on the table?

Referrals should be one of your formal lead strategies. Depending on your business goals and where your business currently is, referrals could become your sole lead source. An endless source of FREE leads significantly adds to the bottom line.

An Endless Flow of Referrals

Let's look at how to build your referral pipeline.

First let's look at the false beliefs that stop people from asking:
- Forgot to ask
- Don't know how to ask
- Waited or were afraid to ask

Let's crush these false beliefs/objections that keep you from asking.

I forgot to ask

"Forgetting to ask" is the same as forgetting to pick up thousands of dollars in profit. You can quickly solve this by starting to formally track how many referrals came in each week and each month. If you see a low number, the solution is to start asking more often. When you have awareness, you suddenly remember. The solution can be as simple as keeping the referral concept in mind. When you remember how important referrals are, you get more of them.

> **PRO TIP:** Want to guarantee you get more referrals? Track how many times you and the team asked for referrals each week.

How to ask for referrals

Don't know how to ask? Or how to properly ask? The solution is to use **Mark's Referral Funnel Formula.**

Mark's Referral Funnel Formula

To get a large volume of quality referrals we need to first and foremost ask for the referral. The other key is to ask effectively, in a way that overcomes the objection of "I'd love to give you a referral, but I can't think of anyone right now." Asking in a manner that creates a "referral funnel" is the solution. This happens when you get your customer to visualize a large number of people, and then they narrow that down to a few people who would be appropriate for you and what you offer.

To best understand how to use this technique, let's review how we helped two different groups of sales representatives get significantly more referrals. One was a group of life insurance agents, and the other was a group of financial planners.

Each group discovered that couples with young children were an excellent prospect. They found that once a couple had children, their priorities became much more focused on future planning and security. So when the agents and planners were presenting to couples with children, we had them sprinkle in a few questions throughout the presentation that got the prospect to disclose several friends who were in a similar stage of life.

1. Have Prospects Think of Their Peers

First, the representatives said something along the lines of, "It is crazy how all of a sudden all your friends are getting married and having children. I bet it seems like only yesterday that everyone was single and thinking so differently." The prospects always agreed, and started thinking about or even mentioning some friends by name that also recently started having children.

2. Have Prospects Compare Themselves to Their Peers

Second, the reps asked a question such as, "Where are *you* compared to your friends in terms of having kids, planning for your first house, etc.?"

At first the prospect was thinking about a large group of their friends and now they are starting to get clearer on who is in a similar situation to them. They are narrowing down the audience.

3. Show Prospects They're Ahead of Their Peers

Next, the representatives pointed out how comfortable their customer must be feeling, having started the process of planning for a solid foundation so early, and what a secure feeling that creates. The prospect always says, "Yes, absolutely," thereby validating to themselves how important it is to be speaking with the representatives and to be taking appropriate action.

4. Have Prospects Imagine Talking About Your Product To Their Peers

Then they ask the prospect which of their friends are going to be most impressed or happiest for them, Or which are going to say something along the lines of "You are really thinking ahead."

At this point, the prospect is typically casually chatting away about who they discuss matters like this with. They even share how they can picture the discussion the next time they see those friends. The prospect even specifically shares information about those friends.

CONGRATULATIONS, they are sharing specifics about another one of your target prospects. They actually know people that can use the insurance or financial planning services. They even mentioned them by name.

5. Ask Prospects To Refer You To Those Friends

Last step, let them know you would be happy to share ways that could potentially help *their* friends too. A*sk for the referral*.

> **PRO TIP:** Have them give you their friends' information rather than passing along yours! That is super important. Even if their friends have the best of intention to call you, many will get busy, forget, or procrastinate. (Although not ideal, you can even assure them that you won't even say where you got their name from. However, that will make the referral less hot.) **The hottest referrals** are the ones where the new prospect has a potential need, you are given the contact information and you can enhance your credibility by mentioning how you helped someone they know.

Stop Waiting *to Ask*

So often people feel they need to *wait* for a variety of reasons. The number one reason is reps and business owners think they need to wait for the product or service to be delivered then used and enjoyed. That is a massive hole in the referral-gathering bucket.

When people first purchase they are thrilled with your product and the idea of buying. If they didn't like the idea of buying, and buying from you, they would not have purchased. You are "their guy." ASK right then.

They may want to wait to give you the referral, but that gives you the opportunity to ask again.

If you choose to wait you may have trouble getting back in touch with the prospect or customer. Even more frustrating is when something goes wrong — even if it is a little thing it often ruins the mood to ask for a referral or shakes your confidence to ask.

For example, I've worked with many contractors. When the homeowner makes their buying commitment they are filled with confidence, so it is a good time to ask for the referral. Another great time to ask is when the job is completed, and they are thrilled. Yet another great time to ask is when you follow up and see how everything is going.

Three opportunities to ask for a referral versus one if you waited. And that one opportunity may not even come if you wait. You get busy, you forget or the prospect is busy and hard to reach.

Make the time to get more referrals. Referrals are very likely to be the lead source with the highest closing percentage and the lowest cost per lead. IN MANY cases, they are FREE.

Should you pay for referrals?

There is nothing wrong with a paid referral campaign, although I firmly believe it is absolutely not required. I refer people to one another because I believe in the service, not for the "kickback" or perk. In many instances, if I'm paid I would feel awkward, and I know other professionals often feel that way too.

Although paying for referrals is not required, that does not mean you should eliminate a paid referral program, or not consider implementing one. Sometimes a paid program makes it more comfortable for staff to ask. In a case where the prospect interactions are more transactional than relationship-driven a paid program can be valuable since there is not a rep interacting with the customer.

The goal is to get MORE LEADS by getting referrals. Keep an open mind toward what could work best for you. Then track performance and let the results be your guide on which solution works best.

Every business can benefit from referrals. If you start asking for them and do so consistently you will get them.

You may be one referral away from an introduction that significantly improves your business.

CHANNEL 3: Strategic Alliances

There are few marketing tools that can have you a) hit a home run, while b) requiring minimal cash and c) minimal risk. STRATEGIC ALLIANCES offer that trifecta.

It is one of the tools that allowed me to significantly grow a digital agency where we managed over 150 digital ad accounts for clients and over 7 figures in ad-spend. Our ad-spend volume and the number of clients even got us invited to Google's Mountain View headquarters in Northern California and their New York City offices in Chelsea.

The client count grew due to utilizing a marketing mix of direct sales, advertising, attending events and getting referrals, but there was one marketing step that was like pouring gasoline on the fire: Strategic Alliances.

Through networking, I received a referral to an organization that became a ***strategic alliance***. The strategic alliance essentially endorsed our agency to each of their clients. They recommended me to ***several hundred*** high quality prospects. This opened the door to me getting connected directly with the decision makers who would authorize the sale. The endorsement was a stamp of approval that made getting the "yes" easier. Each presentation began with our firm already being validated as a credible solution to the prospect's problems.

So be on the lookout for strategic alliance opportunities, and be conscious to add this tool into your marketing mix.

A strategic alliance can take on numerous forms.

It can be as simple as:
- Swapping customer, prospect or lead lists

- Being endorsed to someone's list. (You possibly give a percentage of each sale. You get new prospects and they gain some additional income — possibly even residual income.)
- Getting added to their catalog or resource roster
- Becoming one of their affiliate partners

The strategic alliance is a *win-win* arrangement. Each side brings something to the table that helps the other. It usually has low risk and high potential for a great return.

You have seen many of the world's biggest marketers utilize this tool. Burger King started selling the Impossible Burger. It was a great alliance that gave Burger King a strategic advantage over other fast food chains. It gave their menu a plant-based alternative, which broadened their appeal to a much larger audience. The Impossible plant-based "meat" received more marketing exposure than they possibly could have afforded on their own. Both parties gained sales and exposure.

You have seen movies promoted through strategic alliances with fast food chains. For example, you come in and buy a specific meal and then receive a toy that replicates one of the characters in the movie.

You may have also seen this tool applied in your local market place:
- Bring your ticket stub in after the local sports game and receive a free dessert.
- A local restaurant gives a free dessert if you come in after going to the theatre or the theatre offers something from the concession stand if you come in after going to the restaurant
- A local eyeglass store offers a discount to patients that come from a particular local eye doctor's office. Or on a

grander scale, the eyeglass manufacturer partners with an optometry chain.
- Or a jeweler, florist or wedding photographer collaborate on packages that connect them with additional couples seeking each of their services

What are some possibilities that would work for your business?

CHANNEL 4: Publicity

You and your business need to be known. The more people that know you, the larger your pool of prospects. PR (Public Relations) is a great way to call attention to your business. The right campaign can create huge lead spikes, get people in the door, to your website, and seriously improve sales numbers.

The allure of generating great PR is powerful. How to get it can seem mysterious but it does not require a huge investment. When bootstrapping or in the early stages of testing PR, you can do some of it in-house. As you prove its effectiveness, you might choose to invest in a publicist.

In the early stages of your business a publicist can be very expensive. A rare few work on a pay-for-performance model. You must be very clear about your expectations, the result desired and what you can afford. Till then, remember you can work on generating free PR.

Finding local media lists, regularly reaching out to the local media and crafting a story angle to hook them can be done in-house. Have confidence in your ability to create the sizzle. Recognize you have the ability to create an exciting story.

With a little time and effort you can generate free PR opportunities. As your skills grow you can even reach out to regional and national media contacts. There are many resources that can get you started.

> **PRO TIP:** Before investing in a professional PR firm, learning a bit about how to do it yourself will be very beneficial. Your in-house knowledge will help you hold them accountable to results and maximize their performance. Without that knowledge, you can easily spend thousands per month and get a subpar return.

One of the most valuable aspects of PR is the credibility or social proof it gives you and your firm. PR can be a great source of leads, but repurposing your press clippings can be even more valuable.

When prospects see you have been written up in publications, even small local publications, it separates you from the competition. Prospects often view it as an endorsement, and are instantly more comfortable with you.

Podcasts and local publications need content. If you become familiar with their content needs and their audience and are a good fit to fulfill their content needs accordingly, you can make it a win for everybody. You get free publicity and they get the content they need.

This allowed my firms to get featured in a number of publications. For instance, Telemarketing Magazine was a trade publication that targeted our audience. Each issue always focused on solving a sales or customer service issue. We researched their editorial calendar, saw what themes they had in mind for upcoming issues and then reached out to the editors with article ideas that were in alignment with what they were looking for. It led to us being quoted in various publications and even getting a number of featured-article placements as well.

If you approach editors, producers and podcast hosts with a "give-now, possibly-gain-later" attitude, you will significantly increase your odds of being selected. Those that are only there to promote themselves will be directed to the advertising department, where they are expected to pay to be promoted. If you're a giver you make life easier for the person you are pitching. This in turn will make life easier for you.

One of my coaching clients was a wedding photographer. His client base was local and he knew being featured in the local newspaper would help generate leads. He also knew that it would help his close rate with nervous brides that wanted to be sure each of their vendor selections was perfect. The challenge was that the local publications make their money from advertising and they wanted him to pay. With a little repositioning, we helped him overcome that obstacle.

First we had him learn when the bridal issue was coming out and we contacted the editors several months in advance. Next, instead of focusing on his need for free publicity and asking to be featured in the publication we focused on the editors need for bridal content.

We brought up how every bride wants to look perfect and that we had a story that would play toward that desire. We pointed out how each bride puts a great deal of thought into their dress, hair and makeup, and how each of the people around them looks as well. We played up how many brides even have hair stylists and makeup artists come to their home on the day of the wedding to make sure they look perfect. Naturally the photographer is at the bride's home capturing each aspect of the special day as well. This allowed for several story lines to be presented.

By suggesting a story about how the perfect photographer needs to be invisible to capture the most magical moments of the day, rather than just staging photos, we were able to best serve the editor. The editor wanted content that served the reader. He wanted content that supported his editorial vision. He needed content that would make a valuable guide in which he could sell advertising to people that made money in the wedding industry.

By giving him quality content ideas we made his job easier, and because of that the photographer was able to get featured. The editor ran a story about what a photographer needed to do and not do to capture the essence of each emotion the bride was feeling throughout the entire day. The editor even liked the idea of including photos of local brides getting ready the morning of the wedding, taken by our photographer. Our photographer client was positioned as the expert in the story. A perfect win for everyone involved.

Publicity can be a great tool, and a fun tool, to help grow your business. Just remember it is about service to others first.

CHANNEL 5: Email & Direct Mail

One of your greatest marketing assets is your database of customers and prospects. Utilize it and proactively grow it. Emailing your current and past customers on a regular basis is a marketing must. Anything less is negligent.

E-mail marketing presents huge opportunities for every business. In many cases it is one of the easiest and lowest cost ways to generate repeat business. When someone goes to your website or enters your store, you want to capture their contact information. Every site visitor, every brick

PILLAR 4: Marketing

and mortar visit, is an opportunity to build your database. Create ways to capture the non-buyer contact information. Every name captured is an asset. Offer new products and specials to the people who have visited and/or patronized your business.

Give people a reason to come back. Your specials, your invitations and your educational information are each an effective way to bring people back to your business. Quality offers and educational information will increase repeat visits and grow sales.

Email marketing costs pennies. It is an essential piece of your marketing mix.

Direct mail needs to be approached with much more caution. An excellent response rate is 1% and 1/10 of a percent (0.1%) is common. That means if you send out 1000 direct mail pieces a realistic expectation is somewhere between 1 and 10 people responding. When you calculate postage, production, cost of goods sold and other fees, direct mail can be risky. It can also be highly effective when presenting the right offer to the right list. Just be sure to know your numbers and calculate the minimum response required to breakeven. This will allow you to access risk and rewards.

> **PRO TIP:** The quality of your list and the strength of your offer are essential to how well your direct mail piece will pull.

CHANNEL 6: SEO (Search Engine Optimization)

When we have a question the first place we look for the answer is online. When trying to find a restaurant, a professional service provider, a unique business, a leisure activity or any other widget, we immediately turn to our favorite search engine. When you make your query you get search results and you usually don't read very far down the results page. Meaning you don't go past page one. That means you need to get your business to show on page one for the terms and phrases most relevant to your business.

It is fairly easy to get found when someone is searching specifically for you, i.e. the name of your business. But what happens when someone is not specifically searching for you? When making a more general search, people will see only the businesses that advertise and those that have an effective **Search Engine Optimization** strategy.

Google, Bing and any other search engines make their money on ads. This means the top of the page for each search term goes to paid/sponsored results. But many people skip past those ads. They want something more specific. They have clear search intent. Our goal as 7 Figure Club marketers is to make sure they find us.

Search Engine Optimization is as much art as it is science. Finding a good SEO firm is hard. Many will promise you the world and the presentation will sound great. How can you tell if it is working?

There are several key things to get out of your SEO efforts and they are very trackable.

First, what is your organic website traffic volume and how is it improving? Know your site's traffic levels when you started and watch how it changes monthly. *Note: you should be comparing to the same month in the prior year to account for seasonality.*

Second, make a list of the words and phrases you want to rank for. How many are in the organic positions of #1, the top 3, and the top 10? Each month see how that is improving. It is important to realize that we are more concerned about quality traffic than the number of terms. We also want to make sure the terms being tracked are terms that a significant number of prospects with high purchasing intent are using. Sometimes the SEO firm shows you how your ranking climbed on 100s of terms, the problem is they are not terms most customers will use.

Utilize SEO even though you might not understand it. Good organic clicks typically cost less than paid search clicks, even after including the cost of your SEO agency. Ranking for the right terms can be a game changer. Your SEO experience should be positive as long as you continually measure organic traffic and the number of quality terms you are ranking high for on page one.

> **PRO TIP:** SEO takes time. Be prepared to give your SEO firm three or more months to move the needle. Even when the SEO firm is doing everything right, Google and Bing do not always cooperate. Plus you have your competition working on maintaining their rankings, the same ranking you are looking to take from them.

CHANNEL 7: Telemarketing — An old-school way to get more sales

Telemarketing is still a very powerful and effective sales tool. Every business can benefit from a well-structured telemarketing process. Planning is essential when using telemarketing to generate leads or sales, or enhance customer relations. Getting a positive ROI on your telesales efforts requires more than the right people, the right list and the right "script."

Scripting Note: I believe in *structure* over scripting, which is why my training process is based on teaching your team to *think* rather than blindly follow a script. Call structure and communication structure is far more important than lines on a page.

Telemarketing is not dead but the landscape has changed and we must adjust our approach.

Outbound has gotten ridiculously hard. Inbound, when done right and with proper planning, may have actually gotten easier.

Let's start by addressing why outbound is harder and what can be done about it. Due to automated calls and hidden phone numbers far fewer people are willing to pick up a call unless they actually know who is calling them.

The solution is to call a warm list. Display your company name and let people know who is calling. There are people that actually want what you are offering but won't answer the phone since spam calls have made people suspicious of every call that is unrecognized.

Use the phone to call your customers.

Many small businesses actually have a great relationship with their customers and can leverage that into more sales. Depending on the product or service the reason for the call can be as simple as to just say hello and check in on the client. Those conversations build value, establish connection and often lead to learning about additional needs.

Other businesses can make customer appreciation calls, which are often as simple as saying thank you. Other reasons for a call can be to survey their needs, offer a special bonus, or give them first dibs on something new.

Current customers are more likely to answer the phone, are more receptive to cross-sells and to buying new services. Often overlooked but highly effective is adding reminder calls and welcome back calls to the mix. A happy customer may have stopped buying for a variety of reasons. Calling them to reactivate their accounts or inviting them back to your location can be an easy way to boost sales.

> **PRO TIP:** Telemarketing does not need to be an unwanted cold call. There are lots of reasons for an outbound call to your current customers. Be creative and use outbound telemarketing to build the long-term value of your customers.

Inbound calls are also a function of telemarketing. Many businesses miss making the most of each opportunity. Facebook, Instagram, and email allow you to pop up right in front of your ideal customers. Although targeting them is a bit harder than in the past, it is still way easier than in the "good old days."

A lead can cool rapidly. When customers respond to one of your marketing channels be ready to grab the call immediately. Even returning the call 15 minutes later dramatically reduces your closing percentages. Have a structured plan and process for how inbound opportunities will be handled. Know who will take the call, which questions will be used to uncover the prospects needs, and how the information will be documented. Fuel your growth through preparation rather than winging the presentation. With proper planning you can set your team up for telemarketing success.

Creating Telemarketing Guidelines and Program Structure

Whether you have a small insurance agency with one person generating appointments over the phone or you have enough people dialing on behalf of your sales team to have your own mini call center, you can't just give people a phone and a desk. You need to set them up for success. That happens by pre-planning each of the essential steps.

Break the telemarketing process down into bite size categories. Build a specific checklist of action items and pitfalls to avoid. This will give you a strong framework to grow your business.

Telemarketing 201

The following 69 tips can serve as a roadmap to formalizing your process:

A. Pre-plan the journey and your commitment

1. Know that success is not instantaneous — create a realistic timeline.
2. Write out clear goals and objectives that can be *quantified*.
3. Budget time to manage your people and review their calls.
4. Have a sales training and telesales development process. A sink or swim approach just results in drowning.
5. Set up a productive calling environment. Desk space, computers, noise control, etc.
6. Have a matrix to evaluate successes and what needs improving — Review it WEEKLY.

B. Outsource or Do-it Yourself

7. Either way, each of the planning and review steps must be done regularly.
8. If your prospect list is small and communication is personalized, in-house often best.
9. If data must be reviewed or researched, in-house is essential.

PILLAR 4: Marketing

10. If telemarketing is a major and ongoing pillar of your sales process, in-house.
11. If you are "fishing" for leads and possible prospects, outsourcing might be a better fit.
12. Outsource on short-term projects, especially when short staffed or not properly trained.

C. Know your market

13. Define your best prospect. (Hint: the answer is NEVER "everyone.")
14. Define a qualified prospect as having the money, the need and the authority to say yes.
15. Know the goal of the call — education, research, qualify a prospect, make an appointment, make a sale, etc.
16. Build a good list to call — a quality prospect list is the foundation of your success.
17. Figure out how to create that list — buying lists may be easy but often ineffective.

D. Lead Follow-up

18. Define hot qualified leads.
19. Have a process to move hot leads through the sales channel quickly.
20. Know the cost of waiting to follow up. Hot leads expire faster than a Facebook post.
21. Make sure your sales team is following up promptly.
22. Have process to measure EACH rep's closing percentage on follow-ups.
23. Sometimes the telemarketing is effective but the sales team hinders the efforts.

E. Building your team

24. Who is the right person to manage the telemarketer(s)?

25. Seniority does not guarantee they have the skills to manage callers.
26. List what skills are needed to be effective on calling for YOUR SPECIFIC OBJECTIVE.
27. Personality needed for customer service, appointments, and closing ARE DIFFERENT.
28. Get people experienced on the phone and who like talking.

F. Avoid Turnover

29. Know that many people make a career of telemarketing.
30. Your expectations matter. If you expect telemarketing to fail because you don't like it, it fails. If you believe you are offering value, it works.
31. Create an environment of recognition.
32. Make sure team believes in value of what they promote.
33. Pay people fairly plus additional incentives for success.
34. Have a process to get THE RIGHT PEOPLE FOR PHONE WORK from the start.

G. Training Telemarketers

35. Put the time into training your people.
36. Have a formal training process.
37. Have training: including written procedures, visual education, auditory, and role play.
38. Successful telemarketers pay for themselves 10X+ so invest in them.
39. Know your sales numbers, number of dials, etc. (Good people trained well provide a high ROI.)
40. Formalize the training process — consistency creates predictable results.
41. Make sure the position is viewed as *important* rather than secondary to other sales roles.

H. Equipment Matters

42. Make sure the people have desks, chairs and other needed resources.
43. Sit/stand desks pay for themselves — team more engaged when not always sitting.
44. Learn about predictive dialers.
45. Headset and hands-free is mandatory.
46. Consider cushioned floor mats to minimize fatigue.
47. Software such as a CRM system and other management tools are required.

I. What to Say

48. Know the key point(s) that must be communicated.
49. Know the stages of each call.
50. Know the objective of each stage of the call.
51. Know how to use a script as structured guide.
52. Know how to bring a script to life.
53. Recognize *people* sell, scripts don't.
54. Recognize customers need to be *spoken to*, NOT read a script.
55. Teach your people to engage the customer.
56. Teach your people to get the customer to express their needs.
57. Avoid limiting call length as one of your MAIN objectives.
58. When customers talk they buy — when *spoken at* they don't.
59. The call needs to be long enough for the customer to move forward confidently.

J. Prepare your people to succeed

60. They must practice the presentation.

61. They need to be comfortable with your software and systems.
62. They must plan out their presentation.
63. They must have adequate product knowledge'
64. They must know how to qualify prospects.
65. They must know how to move prospect through the sales process.
66. They need to recognize and act on buying signals.
67. Be ethical, responsible, caring, etc.
68. Have realistic expectations on call volume, success ratios, etc.
69. How to be CONFIDENT.

Make The process FUN and REWARDING

A successful telemarketing program can be a rewarding and fun way to make a nice living for your telemarketers and increase sales for you. It contributes to all parties involved in the transaction.

Following each of the above telemarketing tips will allow you to structure a program that gets a significant ROI.

Build a program you are proud to market, your people are proud to promote and through which your customers gain value from being contacted.

CHANNEL 8: Paid Digital Ads

Whether it is Google, Facebook, Instagram, TikTok, Snap or one of the other digital advertising platforms you need to consider utilizing one or several paid digital ad campaigns as part of your marketing mix.

The key to your success is to know your ROAS as mentioned at the start of this section. If you are getting a profitable return on your ad spend after deducting adverting costs and cost of goods sold from the revenues generated

PILLAR 4: Marketing

from your digital ads you have the opportunity to open up a faucet and fill your leads bucket.

I'm a big fan of having a good understanding of how to do the digital advertising yourself rather than relying on a team member or contractor to do it for you. It may not be practical for you to do it, and you may feel you lack the aptitude to do it, but it is important for you to have a working knowledge of it. This understanding, combined with the tracking of ROAS will keep you from wasting money on approaches that sound good but actually contribute little, if anything, to the bottom line.

There are a number of really good programs. My favorite is the "Certified Advertising Genius Program" offered through *Billy Gene Is Marketing* (**billygeneismarketing.com**). Combine that with their AI program and you will be better prepped to do your own marketing more effectively than many agencies could. Often you are just one ad away from scaling your business and I've found these programs give you the tools to do it. And there are plenty of other options.

As you scale your business to 7 figures you will have numerous departments and vendors. As a 7-figure business owner, rather than operator, it is your role to oversee the success of your digital marketing efforts, and hold others accountable to results.

> **PRO TIP:** Digital ads are highly trackable. Ultimately the number-one stat is knowing the ROAS. If you have a staff person or digital agency that can't answer that easily, then more likely than not you should get rid of them — and FAST. They either don't know what they are doing or they are B.S.-ing you about performance.

Let's look at how to manage your digital efforts rather than operate your digital marketing program:

A medi-spa came to me about scaling their practice. They performed procedures such as Botox, fat melting and other noninvasive cosmetic procedures. The doctor that led the practice told me all about his wonderful Facebook campaigns and Google ads. He told me about the copy that was written and all the clicks he was receiving.

Does this sound familiar?

Have you had someone give you stats that sound good on the surface but don't really tell you anything about profitability? Have you had an agency fill your monthly meeting agenda with exciting creative discussions and then barely touch on your advertising ROI?

That needs to stop.

It is important to know how many clicks/visits you received to your site. It is important to know what position your ads are in and your cost per click BUT all that is meaningless unless you know about the lead and sales numbers.

You MUST know your cost per lead, and your revenues generated from the ads.

In the case of the medi-spa they were not selling products online. They wanted to get patients into the office. In this type of situation you need to know how many visits came into the practice or how many inquiries were generated (emails, inbound texts, calls, or visits). The staff must be taught to find out which lead source brought patients into the practice and then log that information.

If you spend $1000 per week on Google ads and you received 8 inquiries then your cost per inquiry was $125 each. ($1000 divided by 8 inquires is $125.) Essentially that means your *cost per lead* is $125.

If 4 of the 8 inquiries lead to a visit to the practice then you have an *appointment cost* of $250 ($1000 divided by 4 = $250.)

In the case of this medi-spa the average woman coming in spends $600 on the first visit. The medi-spa only made about $300 after the cost of goods sold. Subtract the appointment cost of $250 and they were barely breaking even. However, due to the nature of the service and the wonderful customer service each patient received, they also know that each woman was coming back 6 more times on average. As they returned for massages, follow-up Botox, and other services, another $3600 in sales was generated.

Knowing the numbers made it easy to want to spend more. It was the office's great treatments and customer service that turned a breakeven ad into a moneymaker. Once the staff started asking for referrals consistently, the return generated from the ads grew even higher.

But because they did not have a specific product to track through a sales pixel on the site, the doctor never got an accurate picture of how his ads were performing. The digital-marketing reps would just tell the doctor about cost per click and number of visits. The true marketing pros will be able to explain ways to show you not only the cost per click and the number of visits but the whole story via a CLEAR, REAL, REVENUE-PRODUCING PERFORMANCE MATRIX.

If your performance is based on appointments you should get a dedicated phone number for your ads.

You can clearly track the number of calls received and calculate your cost per call by dividing calls into the ad spend total. Your tracking number should also include recording each conversation so you can grade the quality of the lead. You can also hear how well the staff handled the lead.

Next time you see someone in the car next to you screaming and there is no one else in the car, it might just be a business owner listening to the recordings of how an untrained staff member with no accountability to results was handling an inbound lead. It is funny now, but many business owners were shocked by how calls were handled once they started listening to the calls. Yes, LOL, listening while in their car.

As the owner of your growing 7-figure business it is your responsibility to make sure your staff is trained on how to maximize each lead. Did they make it easy for the prospect to come in? Were they warm and welcoming? Did they make scheduling easy? Did they word things in a way that was positive and solution-focused? Were they using best sales practices? Were they using best customer service practices?

> **PRO TIP:** Leads can be expensive but wasted opportunity can cost a fortune.

If you are selling an actual product online, your webmaster should pop the appropriate tracking pixel onto your site to see ad performance. It is very easy to see what the cost per lead is, and more importantly revenues that were generated from the ad. Did the revenues generated, minus advertising and cost of goods sold create a profit? If so, add fuel to the fire.

As my good friend and great marketer Billy Gene says, "You are only one ad away from making your business explode." When you know ad performance you can test ads, manage advertising providers, and grow your business to the next level.

Selecting the Right Digital Ad Platform - PPC

Your "ad specialist" should also know which advertising platform makes the most sense for your business. Although it can be great to work with someone that specializes in a particular platform I prefer someone that is versed in multiple tools and really has EXPERTISE in each.

Think about it this way: If you have back pain, the chiropractor will say adjustments are what you need, the MD will often use meds as their solution and the surgeon looks toward surgery as the way to solve the problem. It's similar in advertising. I've found Facebook experts think Facebook and Instagram is the answer to everything, a Google Adwords specialist thinks Google is the be-all and end-all top solution and other people think *their* tool of choice is best. Actually, often what they are best at is selling their services rather than advising you on the best tool for your situation. That is why I like a provider that has a big toolbox.

Let's look at home improvement contractors such as plumbers and HVAC specialists. It is true that you can write compelling Facebook ad copy that could inspire a homeowner to use a given contractor, but Facebook is more of "billboard" advertising. You are showing up in front of an audience and trying to inspire them to come to you.

A better option could be if the contractor uses Google Adwords or one of Google's local search tools, then their ad shows up when someone is specifically searching for a solution to a plumbing or HVAC problem. Better yet is when your paid-search specialist puts you into Google Home Service ads. These are ads where you choose to actually pay for the phone call rather than the click. If you know $50 per phone call is a good ROI for you based on call to appointment to sales ratios, you have the opportunity to truly control your lead flow.

I've never had a Facebook specialist tell me about this or recommend anything similar. The moral of the story is get someone versed in multiple options so their agenda is selecting the best solution for you rather than them finding a way to spin their particular specialty to fit your needs.

On the other hand, our medi-spa found Facebook leads converted much better than Google ads. When comparing options, each Google click was expensive and didn't convert since people were often researching other possible solutions. In this case, when compelling Facebook ad copy showed up in their ideal audience's feed, the lead was able to be captured more cost-effectively. The click cost less and the viewer was more compelled to opt in to an offer where they gave their contact info.

You need to test. Then test more. Test a variety of tools that can be tailored to your product or service to position you for growth. Understanding how different tools work for different businesses and for different target audiences is a cornerstone in creating an advertising foundation that yields positive results.

As a business owner, you don't need to know how to do everything but you do need to know the right questions to ask to create accountability from your team. By developing a working knowledge for yourself of how to market with a variety of tools, you are better positioned to lead your marketing department.

PPC Summary

Have your marketing team:
- Explain how cost per call or cost per appointment will be calculated, tracked, and justified.

- Calculate the advertising cost per lead AND per sale.
- Calculate and document ROAS (Return On Ad Spend).
- Explain how often will this be reviewed and how they will show you the numbers.

Channel 9 TRADE SHOWS

Trade shows can be a highly effective way to generate leads, get new clients and gather feedback from your customers. They can also deliver a great ROI — or not. As with most things in business, the profit is in the details.

To make a trade show profitable you must be clear on

a) How you are going to attract people to your booth,

b) How you are going to capture the lead and MOST IMPORTANTLY

c) How you are going to **follow up** with those leads.

I have been to countless trade shows where we had a significant discussion with an exhibitor that qualified us as a prospect, we even told the exhibitor we were interested and we still didn't get a call back after the show.

You must have a **follow-up plan** and you must execute it.

Before even leaving for the show, know who is going to follow up on the leads and have follow-up time **blocked out in the schedule**.

> **PRO TIP:** Leave additional time to call back several times.

Calculate all the costs involved in attending the show and how many customers will be required to make it a profitable show.

Remember, there is more to it than the entrance fee. You have the cost of the show plus airfare, hotel, meals, transportation, trade show displays, graphics and the opportunity costs associated with being out of the office at a minimum.

When selecting a show, try to do some research beforehand. I've found asking my best customers which shows they like to attend to be very valuable. I then ask them why they like the show. Are the people in attendance similar to my best customers? Is the show well attended by my target audience? Does the show format make it easy to meet customers? I've found asking my customers to be a better gauge of the facts than the show's sales reps.

My dad is an excellent example of someone that worked his trade show plan for maximum value. He invented a boom angle indicator for construction cranes. It was essentially the first computer for cranes and would alert the operator if the payload was in danger of flipping over the equipment. Clearly a specialized market.

He knew which shows would be attended by his prospects. He had several deluxe toy cranes he would give away at each show. They were unique, in demand, and they created a buzz. It was a giveaway his prospect wanted and they were happy to trade their contact information for a chance to win it. Part of the genius was that it was 100% relevant to what he was selling. When prospects walked over they spoke about their own machinery. The promotion created rapport with the customer, it qualified the customer and it established meaningful talking points.

Because the conversation was meaningful it led to many appointments being set on spot. Some other people needed to be followed up on. Because they shared details about their situations, my dad was able to make notes, and that allowed for personalized follow-up calls which he blocked time for in his post-show schedule.

The formula: Select the right show, connect with the right prospects, capture their info, and then follow up with them in order to close them. If you can effectively do each of these things for your product or service, then trade shows can be a valuable part of your marketing mix.

Channel 10: PRINT ADS

I've found that print ads can be effective as well as risky.

First let's look at a few of the risks. As we continually transition to digital media the print audience keeps getting smaller. The response of print advertising is also harder to track. Lastly, you pay for circulation, which is not necessarily viewership. Think about how many newspapers and magazines enter your home but go unread.

That said, print can be a great way to target a very specialized audience. The key is to be clear on your objective. Is print part of a bigger branding play? Is it to get in front of an older audience? Is it to reach people when they are researching a particular topic?

Depending on your agenda and needs, advertising in a local publication can work well. In other cases, a trade directory can do wonders. For certain brands, they may need the association that comes from being seen with prestigious brands. Clarity on your agenda is key to your success.

When advertising in print recognize it is all about your headline. If your headline does not grab the reader then your ad won't pull. Your offer also needs to be compelling, and it needs to be seen.

I remember working with a local Chinese restaurant. Their ads always started with the name of the restaurant. The problem was that there were three other Chinese restaurants also advertising in the same publication. In addition to that there were approximately a dozen or more other restaurants advertising in the weekend guide of the publication each week too. Everyone was saying something similar. The name of the restaurant, their cuisine and the basics of what they offered. Food, drink, cocktails, desserts, and catering.

As they grasped the concept of U.S.P. (Unique Selling Proposition) they suddenly had ads that stood out and pulled. If you looked at their menu there were over fifteen entrees that were under ten dollars. That became their ad headline. "Fifteen Meals $9.95 or Less."

Competitors claimed to be a great value but my client was the only restaurant that showed it and proved it. They kept their name big and bold, but moved it to the bottom of the ad because now customers had a reason to read further down. They wanted to see which restaurant was offering such a great value in a crowded market.

Make print work for you by making offers that separate you from the crowd.

> **PRO-TIP:** If you can't *make a great offer* then question if you have an offer that is worth advertising. So much of your marketing success comes down to your offer. The better the offer the better the results, as long as you put that offer in front of a qualified audience.

Marketing Channel Summary

By now I'm hoping you see how various marketing channels can help support one another.

As you network with other professionals you generate low-cost leads that allow you to get sales without needing to spend lots of money on marketing.

Your wonderful customer service and excellent value make it easy to get referrals.

Each channel increases sales. *Profitable* sales give you the extra cash flow needed to experiment with a variety of paid advertising.

Multiple channels are recommended to scale your business into a profitable 7-figure business.

Marketing takes many forms

There are so many different ways you can attract people to your business. Television, radio, speaking circuit, flyers, fairs or expos, billboards, barter, signage, workshops, lunch-and-learns, premium incentive items and events are among your options. We can make the list even longer. The key to evaluating which tool you should use to continue to grow is to always stay focused on evaluating your Return on Ad Spend.

We focused on 10 marketing channels that give you both diversity and control over your lead flow. They have either lower costs with a high rate of return for your efforts, or are highly trackable thus helping you continually leverage your Return on Investment.

7 Figure Club businesses have multiple channels to continually fuel growth in a variety of markets. Most importantly a 7 Figure Club business owner manages the team and their accountability to stats that show they are being effective.

Multiply Your Growth Rate

There are three main ways to grow your business:

The first is getting new business. This is the one most business owners seem to focus on. Possibly because it was the first one they needed when first starting out. Although continually bringing in new business is essential, having that be your sole focus is short sighted.

The second thing to do is increase your average transaction value. Find ways to increase the value of each transaction by 10% to 20%. This is a realistic goal for almost every business. Often you can even increase the order value by far more.

Third, your repeat order rate is essential to really increase sales and the profitability. Find ways to keep the customer coming back with great offers, delivering a great value and great customer service. Great service can be the easiest and most cost-effective way to keep the customer away from competitors and continually coming back to you.

As a business owner and as a member of the 7 Figure Club, your focus is on growth as well as profits.

You have the process to sell.

You have the process to get an abundance of quality leads.

Do all the above three things simultaneously while delivering an award-winning level of customer service and your business will rapidly scale.

PILLAR 5
CUSTOMER SERVICE
— THE SECRET SAUCE

Customer service can be the tailwind that accelerates your growth. It creates raving fans and brand ambassadors, those customers that come back to buy again and again, which equals MORE REFERRALS too.

Harnessing the power of marketing, sales and great customer service is the trifecta that will grow your business tremendously. Even more importantly, once you master combining the three you can weather any storm and recover from devastating blows. Outstanding customer service is that special ingredient required to build your business bigger and better.

Ryan Treadwell of Kona Contractors, a home improvement firm in Denver Colorado, is a perfect example of this. Ryan was a natural at selling. As good as he was, he was even better at learning ways to continually improve and grow.

In each aspect of business, he continued to learn and he started his own enterprise. He was able to grow it rapidly and profitably.

Then the real estate market turned and he was hit with a massive downturn. While other home improvement firms folded, Ryan was able to weather the storm and was able to come back even stronger than before. More often than not the climb higher and higher is never straight upwards. Sometimes there are some nasty downturns that come in many forms.

Unfortunately, market headwinds caused Kona Contractors to lose a significant portion of its business. In his early forties and hit with a big setback, Ryan could have just chugged along and still done very well by many business owners' standards. However, Ryan knew the 7 Figure Club Success Formula and was 100% positive and crystal clear that he would have it all back and he would do so quickly. In only three years he became the premier outdoor beautification contractor in Colorado. He set an even higher standard for himself and grew the business well into the 7 figures, and is on track to surpass that.

What was his secret and where is the gold?

To establish 7 Figure growth we need to generate quality leads. Closing those leads is of course also required. But Ryan and every 7 Figure Club business owner will tell you that none of it is sustainable without a concentrated focus on customer service.

Simply put: Raving Fans come back again and again. Raving Fans tell their friends too. It is just too hard, expensive and difficult to continually market, to always be finding new customers.

Repeat business and larger transactions are where you find the gold. Both of those require a great reputation built on A.N.A.W.A.R.D.™ Winning Level of customer service.

Let's look at Ryan's contracting business.

He is selling a big-ticket luxury product. It is also a complicated product. Whether you are remodeling, doing

PILLAR 5: Customer Service

a major renovation or building something from the ground up, there is a lot that can go wrong. You are also dealing with a demographic that has a very high standard and is used to getting things their way. On top of that it is their home you are working on and that can be stressful and filled with emotion.

Obviously, customer service issues are going to come up.

Let's take a particular homeowner that had a delay due to the local municipality being slow to issue permits, then when work was started the homeowner did not accurately communicate what they wanted and there were some hidden structural issues to complicate things further.

Ryan and his team know these things are bound to happen. They are faced with them daily and are fully capable of solving them but each little bump is a new frustration for the homeowner. Customer service is key to keeping everyone calm and patient.

Rather than the customer being wrong for communicating their desires incorrectly it was viewed as an opportunity to educate. Each member of the crew introduced themselves when they saw the homeowner or a family member. They were not strangers or workmen, they were guests.

They actively listened when someone made a request so the customer continually felt heard. They were thoughtful in their choice of words and language used in the household. They were always mindful of the fact that construction and renovations are putting someone's home in a disorganized state, which increases the likelihood of someone being "stressed out."

When every member of the Kona Contracting family, from receptionist to construction crew to admins and executives, maintains this level of mindfulness, customers have an exceptional experience.

Ryan's secret was to instill in each and every member of the team that *we all do whatever it takes to make the customer happy*. Customer service is everybody's responsibility. Every member of an organization's staff is part of the customer service department.

This mindset led to happy customers, great reviews, a fantastic reputation, lots of referrals and lots of repeat business.

You can build a business on a great product and great customer service. Always remember you need both.

Who is your customer service team?

EVERYONE.

Each member of your team plays a role in customer service. Establish a corporate culture where each and every member of the team represents that department. Everyone contributes to what people say about your company.

Make sure your entire team recognizes that the customer is more likely to vent about a frustration to friends, family, coworkers, and strangers rather than your personnel. When they do share an issue with members of your team, you must remember that the customer is also telling 10 other people about the issue too. And if we include social media posts that number is significantly higher.

> **PRO TIP:** The number of people that can hear about a frustration is multiplied 10-fold because those friends and family members your customer told are also telling others about the experience.

Let's not overcomplicate it:
EVERY STAFF MEMBER is customer service.
Every interaction is customer service.
How the phone is answered is customer service.
How you offer, and hand someone a cup of coffee or a bottle of water is customer service.
How you enter someone's home and how workmen put down protective floor mats is customer service.

Every interaction with the customer should be seen as a customer service interaction.

> **PRO TIP:** A customer is significantly more likely to tell others outside your organization about something that bothered them than about something they loved. They will also go out of their way to express a frustration to more people than to sing praises. Therefore each *time you hear a customer complain take it seriously.* Customers expect excellence. Customers *deserve* excellence and they *should* expect it. If ever in doubt, think about when you are the customer and you will quickly recognize the customer's viewpoint of great service is the expected standard.

Dealing With Difficult Customers

Difficult customers can test even the best of your customer service personnel.

The most effective way to deal with a difficult customer is through "active listening." It is not always easy to calmly listen to the difficult customer, but it is effective. When the customer is talking loud or forcefully, they are trying to make themselves heard. High volume and harsh tone is usually a sign of their frustration and communicates that they do not feel understood.

In the heat of the moment it can be challenging to feel empathy for this individual. Recognizing how they are feeling even though you don't like how they are expressing it is the first step to hearing them more effectively.

Clear communication comes out of really making an effort to listen and understand customers. The ability to listen is greatly increased when you can separate yourself from the situation and realize it is not about you. The ability to make someone feel heard and understood can disarm even the most heated of situations.

Get the focus off of the complaint. Challenging situations escalate and then erupt because both the difficult customer and the person trying to help them are spending too much time reliving the problem.

Ninety percent of the effort must be on finding a solution rather than focusing on the problem. Quickly get the conversation onto discussing solutions, and keep the focus on moving toward a solution that you can implement. All while continuing to have the other party feel heard and understood.

The Three Solutions Rule

It is important to focus on solutions over problems. When the majority of a conversation is about problems it is very draining on your staff and also on the customer. When the focus is on the problem most of the energy is on placing blame, or giving reasons why things are incorrect. This makes everyone more uncontrollable and the situation more heated.

When the focus is on solutions, everyone is happier because the energy is on making things right. It is much more pleasant to look at the good rather than the bad.

After getting a handle on the customer's viewpoint, we can help a very difficult customer gain a sense of control by suggesting multiple solutions. The act of their choosing between multiple solutions gives them something positive to control. Rather than their focus being on the problem, they are now choosing between solutions. Even when the solution is imperfect it is still a better area of focus than what was wrong.

Suggesting options in a helpful positive tone, combined with giving your customers choices, positions you as someone that is on their side. The customer can happily choose one of the options, or they may make suggestions about how to adjust what was presented.

Either way we have shifted the difficult customer from an adversary to someone with whom we are working to craft a pleasing outcome. The representative feels good that they are guiding the customer to a solution. The customer feels empowered because they are participating in how their problem is being resolved. Together, they come up with a solution that seems sensible.

A.N.A.W.A.R.D.™ Winning Level of Service

Having your customer truly feel special is actually rather easy. Regardless of your industry, you can get your team to turn even the most difficult customer into one that sings your praises.

The key is in making them feel both heard and significant. By having your team focus on our 7 core communication principles during each customer interaction they can make your ratings skyrocket.

By following each of the 7 principles outlined in A.N.A.W.A.R.D.™ you will disarm irate customers.

By avoiding the common mistakes that spark a customer's argumentative side, many calls will become more pleasant.

When customers recognize your effort to align yourself with their viewpoints, confrontations will be minimized and solutions will be achieved more rapidly. Best of all, you can take pride in helping someone, and in a job well done.

Set a standard for your team. That standard is that your organization is fully committed to delivering "An Award" Winning level of service.

To meet that standard, we don't just say it. We live it and communicate it to each and every customer by assigning meaning to each letter of our deliver "An Award" winning level of service mantra.

Each letter of A.N.A.W.A.R.D.™ has significance

A. Avoid making the customer wrong
N. Name Power: Names humanize the individuals
A. Ask customers what they want
W. Words chosen change feelings
A. Affirm you heard them
R. Realize the good in your life
D. Delete BUT, HOWEVER, and TRY from your vocabulary

Let's look at each piece of A.N.A.W.A.R.D.™ in greater detail:

A: Avoid Making The Customer Wrong

Even if the adage "The customer is always right" is not always true, it is important to avoid making them feel they are *wrong*. People will argue to avoid being wrong. One of the easiest ways to avoid a battle of who is right and who

PILLAR 5: Customer Service

is wrong is by never placing blame. Keep a customer from becoming defensive by never actually using the words "You're wrong."

Customers will be wrong. We've all experienced that time and time again. Just don't say it. The words "You're wrong" makes people get defensive. Stop and notice how you feel when people say those words to you. Even when you are wrong and you know it, you don't like being called out on it.

Allow your customer to "save face" by not actually using those words.

The easiest way to do that is just to avoid starting your explanation with the words "You are wrong." Ideally, just give the correct explanation without using the "W" word.

A gentle buffer that allows you to show empathy and shift the conversation to the correct explanation is to start with a phrase such as:

- I can see how you would think that
- Many people also initially thought that
- At first, I also thought that
- Or some other non-judgement-oriented statement

Frequently customers argue because they are positive they are right. They genuinely believe it.

We had a customer that wanted to use a 10% off coupon on one of my business's websites, **www.BulkOfficeSupply.com**.

The item they were purchasing was already discounted and the coupon was only for first-time customers. The coupon clearly stated that which is the reason it would not work: It was for first-time customers and this customer already made purchases in the past. They called complaining that the coupon did not work. They gave us the code, told us where they got it, claimed they never ordered before and insisted that the coupon code didn't say for first-time customers.

We were able to see their name, address, and email in the system along with an order history. Clearly they had ordered before. We also could see the banner with the promo code and wording stating it is for first-time customers.

Telling the customer they were wrong or even mistaken is not going to score points, build loyalty or promote an internal culture of *An Award Winning Level of Service*. Instead, we simply pointed out how easy it is to not recall all the sites each of us buy from.

We even made it easier to save face by mentioning that someone else from their organization may have placed the other orders. We emphasized options rather than criticize, or make them wrong.

We appreciated their coming back and educated them on it being a one-time code for new customers. Then we happily let them know we were processing the discount manually, thanked them and let them know we look forward to them being a long-term customer of BulkOfficeSupply. com and benefiting from our big discounts.

There is much more value in planting the seed for future business, promoting the selling point of the bulk discount, and cultivating the relationship than winning the battle of who is right and wrong.

The skill, the value and the win are in being right about maintaining long-term repeat customers.

_____

_____

_____

N: Name Power

A difficult customer is often someone who is asserting themselves in order to feel important and in control. By making them feel important without them becoming assertive keeps all parties calm and relaxed. When you ask a customer their name they see that you are taking an interest in them as an individual, and that makes them feel special. The more you address them by their name, the more they will feel important.

A person's name is the sweetest sound to them, and each time you use it they realize you are making an effort to work with them.

> **PRO TIP:** Also give *your* name. It accomplishes several things. First of all, your client or customer feels in control. They know who they are talking to, and that they are not just talking to a robot. The personal touch of a name gives substantially more credibility to your solution and importance.

Most importantly, when you use names you are no longer strangers. That makes it a bit easier for everyone to stay even-tempered. People want to work with people. Knowing *their* name and using it, plus having them know and remember *your* name, humanizes the entire interaction.

It is much more enjoyable for customers to come back to a business where they feel they know the people. They are made to feel more significant when they feel they are known. Many people crave a sense of community. When your customers know you and you know them, you have taken a major step toward building the feeling of community that builds a history of repeat business.

How can you get your team to have customers know who served them?

In what situations can they learn, and utilize the customer's name?

How can you utilize the power of name power to build your customer community?

___

___

___

A: Affirm Understanding

Make sure you understand your customer correctly.

It is very frustrating when a customer service matter is not fully understood. It is hard on both the customer and the person working toward an acceptable solution.

Paraphrase the customer's problem. By paraphrasing it, they will have tangible proof that you are trying to see their viewpoint. After restating a customer's problem add, "Is that right?" or "Is that everything?" That gets them to say "yes," and see that you really did hear everything they said.

When the customer affirms that you understand their needs and issues, you have them recognizing that you are working with them in a positive manner. As conversation progresses in that direction, all parties feel satisfied that something is getting accomplished. This results in everyone staying calm and content while focusing on the solution.

> **PRO TIP:** The customer may let you know that you didn't fully understand everything. That is also great. It is better to have them share more information and get you 100% on the same page about the situation rather than attempt to solve something by going down the wrong path or an incomplete path.

How can your team do a better job of actively listening and restating the issue to the customer?

How can they utilize fully-hearing what the customer is saying to help create solutions that leave the customer feeling complete, satisfied and fully heard?

_____

_____

_____

W: Wording

Our words

Angry, unreasonable and obnoxious are words that remind us of very difficult customers. When we describe certain customers with these words, the vision in our mind often makes us tense and has our blood pressure increase.

We can trick our mind into a calmer state by referring to these customers as *challenging* or *needy*. When you use words that have softer connotations your mind defines the situation as softer. Changing the words you use to refer to your difficult customers will help you maintain a more relaxed state.

> **PRO TIP:** You can also use the technique when paraphrasing a difficult customer's situation as you work to tone them down.

The customer's words

When a customer uses very negative language to express a feeling or to describe a solution, soften the language when affirming what you heard. If they said something was horrible, you can repeat back that you clearly hear something was not to their liking and you want to remedy the situation. That shifts the mindset off of something being "horrible," and has them hearing your solutions.

Those very difficult customers really just want to know they were heard and that someone is finding a solution. Your choice of wording is a major step toward creating that feeling and shifting their focus.

How can you have each member of the customer service team be more focused on how they reframe what the customer is saying?

How can they combine using "softer" words with each of the previous elements of A.N.A.W.A.R.D.™ to enhance the customer experience in difficult situations?

_____

_____

_____

A: Ask them what they want

It's amazing how often customer service reps neglect to ask a customer what they specifically want.

PILLAR 5: Customer Service

Customers will often express their complaints passionately and then only give a vague description of what they are looking for in terms of a solution. This is frustrating for both the customer and the representative. When frustration builds, everyone becomes more uncomfortable.

When a customer service representative learns the specific needs that must be met to satisfy a customer there is a solid foundation for finding a solution. The solutions are often simple and the frustration easily avoided if you just ask them what they want.

People often just need to be heard. Sometimes they just want to have their view or their experience validated. When we ask the customer "What do you want?" or "What would you like?" their requirement is often very easy to accommodate.

We were working with the front desk staff of a hotel. Frequently the biggest challenges they faced could easily be solved by genuinely listening while smiling sincerely. When the customer was asked what we could do to make up for "it" they often didn't know. In many cases they even said "We don't need anything, we just wanted to call 'it' to your attention." Sometimes the front desk staff just replied, "Thank you for letting us know Mr. ____. That feedback is helpful and appreciated."

Using the customer's name and repeating back what was shared in a calm and friendly manner was all it took to shift the mood. The customer felt validated and significant. Sometimes a voucher for an in-room movie, breakfast or a snack from the convenience mart would be offered. In every instance the goal was to have the customer feeling acknowledged and taken care of. The staff was clear each interaction is an opportunity to deliver *An Award Winning Level of Service*.

> **PRO TIP:** Embrace asking the customer what they want. The vast majority of people will make at most a modest request. Often the answer is nothing; they just wanted someone to know about the situation. You are then in the perfect position to do a little something for them. Suddenly you become the problem solver as well as the staff person that gave them extraordinary service.

How can you empower your team to solve problems without needing to ask for a manager?

How can you help them to better understand the value of granting the customer's request in order to build loyalty, positive word of mouth and repeat business?

_____

_____

_____

R: Realize the good in your life

When dealing with an unruly customer, step back and realize their behavior may be driven by extraordinary circumstances. Being grateful for your own life can help keep you centered in these situations.

Some customers can be unreasonably difficult because of issues that have nothing to do with you. Their life might be complicated by divorce, health problems or financial crisis. They can take the stresses of their life out on any individual that crosses their path.

We've all had a bad day. When we do, we often express things harshly. Often that communication is directed at

PILLAR 5: Customer Service

someone who doesn't deserve it. Recognize that the difficult customer you are helping may just be having a bad day.

Keep it simple: What they are upset about probably has nothing to do with you so don't hold onto that negative vibe. Let it go.

> **PRO TIP:** Don't take the negative vibes that are directed towards you personally. Most importantly, count your blessings and realize all you have to be thankful for.

How can you help your team stay focused on the positive and not take customer complaints personally?

Is there a notoriously *challenging* customer you work with whose attitude you can reframe or find a new way to appreciate them?

While I was helping the customer service personnel of a medical cannabis dispensary, the approach of "realize the good in your life" proved very helpful for the team. They had many customers that seemed to never smile. Certain customers were always grouchy and the staff viewed them as difficult customers. But the reason they were grouchy was because the customers (aka patients) were in chronic pain. These customers were often under a doctor's care and they were coming to the dispensary to refill their prescriptions.

Once the dispensary staff was reminded that these people had serious conditions that literally took the smile off their faces and the bounce out of their step, the staff was filled with compassion. They now realized the negative energy was not aimed at them personally. This shift in understanding allowed them to be more gracious servers. They realized how helpful they were being and began to treat those patients/customers with extra kindness.

We don't know everything our customer is experiencing.

Recognize all you have to be grateful for. Your situation may be far better than the person you are serving and you can always take pride in your ability to treat everyone with kindness.

_____

_____

_____

D: Delete "but" "however" and "try" from your vocabulary

The words "but" and "however" negate any positive comments you may make to help calm a difficult customer. For example, if someone told you "I love what you are wearing, *but* those shoes don't match," the only thing you hear is that the shoes don't match. The compliment is completely overshadowed.

The same is true in customer service.

If you tell a customer "I want to help, *however* that is not my job/department" the only thing the customer hears is that you will not help.

Avoid escalating heated situations with the words *but* or *however*. They only make your customer or client feel you are being confrontational. Even worse, they'll feel that you are saying they are wrong and you won't help.

How about when a customer wants a refund or an exchange? The customer is told "I really want to help BUT/HOWEVER the company policy does not allow adjustments after 30 days." Does that customer hear "I want to help?" Of course not. They hear "No."

PILLAR 5: Customer Service

How about when you are the customer and you are suddenly the one hearing "I'd love to help you BUT it is not my job." Or they tell you "I really want to help, HOWEVER I'm still on my break or just got off duty." You probably don't like it. In each case the words *but* or *however* erased the kind words that came before them.

There are times when we can't give the customer what they are requesting. We do need policies and guidelines.

What we want to recognize here is we don't want to negate the positive of what we are saying with the use of "but" and "however."

The solution is easy. Just replace "but" and "however" with the word "and" or by a pause before making your second point.

For instance a customer wants to order more food from the kitchen after it has closed and cleaning has begun. In the past, the wait staff might have said they would be happy to place that order BUT/HOWEVER the kitchen is already closed.

We can practice the skill of deleting the use of but and/or however by saying something like "I'd be happy to place that AND unfortunately the kitchen just closed." Or "I'm so happy you enjoyed everything, (pause) unfortunately the kitchen is already closed."

There are numerous ways you can communicate less-than-ideal news to a customer without using but or however. Get used to deleting "but," "however" and "try" during easier interactions and it will be habit when faced with a more challenging situation.

Remember to deliver your message politely, with a pleasant tone and thoughtful wording.

The word "try" is verbalizing a form of self-defeat before you even start. It is setting the expectation that what you are "trying" may not be achieved. Instead, be confident. Be affirmative. Let the customer know you will do everything you can within your authority.

Be a person of action. Let the customer know you are on it, and will personally follow up with them. You are not promising the result, and at the same time you are taking ownership on behalf of the customer.

"Do" rather than "try."

Help your team have fun developing the habit of eliminating *but*, *however*, and *try* from their vocabulary: Have your team brainstorm how removing those three words will help improve the customer's experience.

___

___

___

Enrolling Your Team in A.N.A.W.A.R.D.™

In each of my organizations, every member of the team has the authority to do something for the customers. The nature of their role and how long they have been in that role will define what they are authorized to do. At a minimum everyone has the authority to solve a problem immediately if all they need to do is offer a "perk" of $25 of less. Some team members can go as high as $500 without needing a manager to get involved. The value of a happy customer along with the value of a team that takes pride in taking ownership of a problem and solving it far surpasses the expense.

Empower your people to truly give A.N.A.W.A.R.D.™ winning level of service.

Be Known for Your Customer Service Excellence

A business that develops a culture of A.N.A.W.A.R.D.™ winning level of service has customers that tell stories about the excellent service received.

La Cantinaccia del Popolo is a lovely restaurant in Sorrento, Italy. They start serving dinner at 7 p.m., which is early for Italy. A line starts to form at 6:30 p.m. before they are even opened. If you come at 8 p.m. you are going to have a long wait and they don't take reservations.

The owner is taking care of the people in line before they even enter, before they are even his customers. He will periodically take trays of appetizers or plastic cups with a little wine out to the folks on the line. It is his gracious treat to those patiently waiting. He also introduces himself and connects with the people waiting.

Instead of the line being a frustration, he has turned it into part of the customer experience. And if anyone fills their stomach before they can enter it only shortens the wait for the next person in line. He is fully present in the act of serving his customers.

Oh, and those folks who left the line after a few free treats? (If anyone ever does.) They probably told 10 of their friends about the great experience.

> **PRO TIP:** Brainstorm with your staff ways to create a great customer service experience. What are the customer service stories you can be known for? Have the team suggest solutions that can help them go from *trying* to improve to *committed* to improving **now**.

A.N.A.W.A.R.D.™ Winning Level of Service is never an expense. It is always a great investment that offers a huge return for everyone.

Nordstrom has so many customer service stories it is hard to separate fact from fiction. There are stories of customer service personnel refunding tires when Nordstrom didn't even sell tires, the place next to them did. Is it true, who knows? What we do know is in retail they are the known as the king of customer service.

Marketing may bring people to your business. Having what the consumer needs and having good sales skills that communicate value will close more transactions. It is customer service that will keep them coming back.

Create a culture of A.N.A.W.A.R.D.™ winning level of service and continually deliver on it. You will gain an abundance of 5 Star reviews. More importantly, you will gain an abundance of repeat customers that become the foundation of your highly profitable 7 Figure Club Business.

PILLAR 6
NEGOTIATION —
BECOMING A MASTER

When are you making $1000 per minute?
When you are negotiating.
                    Mark Anthony

Negotiation is essential. It is one of your most valuable skills and one where few business owners have a structured formula. As your business grows, you will find the need to negotiate becomes more and more important. It is a powerful skill to develop. Although many people find negotiation intimidating, it becomes easy once you shift your viewpoint about how to be an effective negotiator.

Instead of seeing the person opposite you as an adversary, shift the paradigm to that of you playing a game with an opponent, or solving a puzzle. Mentally you will go from someone *preparing for a fight* to someone *preparing for a game*. Notice the word **preparing** — most of your negotiation success comes from your preparation rather than what you say.

Games are something you can look forward toward, you embrace the opportunity to play, and actually enjoy it. A fight has many of the opposite connotations. Even those that enjoy a fight know it is usually best to avoid them.

Whatever your current view of negotiation, you need to get good at it. There will be countless opportunities to negotiate. Literally every single day. Although they won't all be major negotiations, recognizing you are constantly faced with negotiations is an important key to your success. If you notice you have the opportunity to negotiate daily, you will recognize the numerous opportunities to practice negotiating daily. Step into this opportunity. If you start to negotiate each time you have the chance, you will build your negotiation muscles and be MUCH more comfortable for the real negotiations, the negotiations with a significant price tag attached to them.

Getting good at negotiation will make you hundreds of thousands over your business career and likely **MILLIONS**. As your business grows you will have to negotiate leases, employment agreements, labor issues, a wide variety of contracts and, most of all, sales.

When is your time worth $1000 per minute or even more?

When you're negotiating!

I was helping a client in the garment business who was growing so rapidly she could no longer keep up with the production of the light summer dresses she designed. Her creative cuts and trendy designs, combined with spot-on marketing, had orders coming in faster than her team could make them. A great problem to have but a logistical nightmare. It was taking her off her core competencies of design and marketing. Growth was literally becoming a frustrating stressful distraction.

So we looked into outsourcing. We found a vendor we were very comfortable with. We walked in knowing our

PILLAR 6: Negotiation

current costs and how our costs would change if we kept expanding production in house. We also knew the numerous opportunity costs involved with keeping it in-house under her roof.

The supplier wanted $15.00 per dress which was crazy. Her current costs were about $8.00. This was far too big a jump to pass onto customers. If her company absorbed the increase it would kill profit margins.

> **PRO TIP:** Once again, notice the importance of knowing your numbers.

$10.00 was the perfect number. It matched our projected in-house cost increases and if someone else did the production it would make expanding much easier, allowing for even more growth with far fewer headaches. Wow, the dream scenario!

The vendor was certain they couldn't get anywhere near our $10.00 price target.

With some brainstorming focused on solving the pricing problem, the tone of the negotiation was one of mutual success. It was much more effective than one side trying to beat the other up on price.

By helping them get clearer on what we needed and us getting clearer on their production bottleneck concerns, we started finding ways to solve each other's issues that were barriers to bringing the price down. As the discussions progressed we uncovered even more adjustments we could make on our end in terms of timelines. That allowed the supplier to come down even further.

They could get the price down to $13.00 per dress. A bit more than we wanted but reasonable. We knew it was a realistic price and the benefits gained in terms of stress reduction and growth capacity were worth the extra $3.00 even though that added up to $100K in increased cost.

In our discussions, I got this savvy businesswoman to push back. Once we were united, we told the manufacturer it really just wouldn't work and that we really needed them to come in at a lower number. We discussed $11.75. It still seemed a little high, but internally we asked ourselves if we could live with it. The answer, YES. And YES was the outsourcing company's answer too.

The additional $1.25 savings added up to $50K per year based on her volume at that time. On the spot, in a 10-minute conversation $50K per year was saved. Pushing, staying fully engaged in the game, embracing the discussion with our "opponent" rather than running away from the awkwardness of pushing back on a supplier we liked, was worth $5K PER MINUTE. Later that year the business continued to grow significantly. The extra $1.25 a unit was actually worth closer to $100K SAVINGS in year one. That was an ongoing ANNUAL SAVINGS that actually grew as the unit volume grew.

Remember, there are many negotiating opportunities where your time is worth $1000s of dollars per minute!

When is negotiating worth $1000 or more per minute?

- When in real estate deals — $1000s per minute
- When in employment discussions — $1000s per minute
- When working with suppliers or vendors — $1000s per minute
- And of course when you are closing sales — $1000s per minute

Build Your Negotiation Muscle Daily

When you negotiate more often, you are ready when you are confronted with big negotiations. I travel frequently for both business and pleasure. As many as 20 weeks per year.

I don't need a free movie with my stay or a coupon for a complimentary breakfast but I ask EVERY TIME. It is a mini negotiation opportunity:

As I approach the reception desk, I proactively greet the reception person at the hotel with a warm smile and a big hello. I ask them how they are doing and thank them for their friendly greeting at whatever early or late hour it happens to be. I let them know how happy I am to be back or what great things I heard about the hotel from others. With each step I am intentionally building rapport as well as increasing my value as a customer.

As they work on check-in I ask about room upgrades, late check out, maybe a cocktail to relax after my long flight, and breakfast. I usually don't ask for every item, but I select a few. Sometimes I get all of them, sometimes a few and almost always at least one. It is important to recognize that three out of four times they say, "I'm sorry, I can't do that." I'm playful and with a smile say "Of course you can, come on, I'd really appreciate it." Depending on my mood I might point out in a very friendly tone that "the Double Tree gives me a warm cookie at check in, see what you can do." And at least half the time I get some little perk.

Let's be SUPER CLEAR: The value here is not in getting a $15 breakfast voucher. The value is in *building the muscle* of being willing to ask for a concession from my "opponent."

I've learned that when they say "no" nothing bad happens. I've also learned that when I don't ask, *nothing happens*, and when I do ask I often get exactly what I ask for or at least more than if I stayed silent. The two minutes spent asking usually gets me something worth at least $15. Hey, $7.50 per minute is $450 per hour, right?

Seriously, building the muscle of being willing to ask, and having a strategy behind how you ask, is essential. You need to build the muscle before you need it. Prepare for the negotiation opportunities before they arrive. It will literally save you and/or make you a minimum of tens of $1000s, more times than you can count.

The kid takes on the seasoned PRO

Possibly my favorite negotiating story is regarding a licensing agreement I had with one of the oldest and most prestigious schools in New England. At the time, I had my sports publishing company where we produced game programs for college football and basketball games. These were very similar to the game day programs you would get if you attended a pro event. We made our money primarily through the sales of program advertising.

Three years earlier, when I first acquired this prestigious university as a client, their game program was nothing more than a flyer. It was a sheet of paper folded in half to create 4 pages. There was a cover page with some event info about the day's game, a page for the home and visiting team's roster, and the back page was the schedule and continuation of the cover story. That was pretty much it.

They knew it was subpar compared to the game day magazines sold at their competitors' arenas. They needed something much better than that and I had an established track record of taking a school from nothing to a full-fledged magazine fast. Our first meeting was quick and they were ready to sign right away. We set up a 3-year agreement.

Everything went great and we delivered a 48-page, glossy magazine with photos of each player, stories about the school and game-day features, along with prestigious advertisers that elevated the overall look of the publication.

Then the mood changed. Season four was about to start, the contract had expired and my communication with Jim, the director who oversaw my area, was no longer giving me a warm and fuzzy vibe. You know that point in a relationship when you can tell something is up? Well it was and I could tell. Even worse, Jim called a meeting. He said, "We need to talk." He wanted to discuss the contract and I had a feeling it wasn't looking good.

He represented the prestigious university and believed that I should be honored to work with them and privileged to have them as a marquee client. On top of that he pointed out that I was making good money on the account.

Now that they had a substantial and established magazine, other sports publishers wanted the account. They were knocking on his door. They were bigger firms. The director wanted the bigger firm now. After all, his university was as prestigious as you can get and shouldn't be represented by a kid and his little firm. I was about 23 at the time.

We had our meeting, and as I've mentioned in both sales and negotiation, your power comes from your preparation, your planning and knowing your numbers. So plan and prep is exactly what I did.

Now part of the fun (notice that mindset) was that he was this established, gruff older guy. A real tough persona. He liked to negotiate and he liked to take a hard line, an in-your-face approach. One of my greatest assets was that I knew that going in.

I walked in and he got right down to it, telling me all the reasons it was time to move on to another firm. It was a good ride but now it was over. He just thought I at least deserved to hear it face to face. His assistant Bill was there to observe how being a tough negotiator is done. How you set the stage for the best deal, one-sided terms, etc.

My response, I looked him straight in the eyes, reached into my briefcase and pulled out his "game program" from 3 years earlier. That little piece of paper — a flyer. In a strong, somewhat confrontational tone I told him, "Your university name did nothing to build up your magazine. You essentially had nothing, except for an embarrassment of a flyer before my firm and I took on the project. I showed him what he had and literally threw in on his desk. It was so light and flimsy it floated onto his desk. Then I showed him what we created. A magazine with color, content and weight. I threw the latest issue onto his desk. Bam, it had weight and substance. Then I pulled out another one of his old issues and another one we created. I stated here is what you created compared to what we created. I looked him in the eye and confidently let him know there was no comparison.

Be Confident

We each did some verbal pushing and posturing back and forth. He had someone standing up to him. Someone pushing back. Game on!

Now before things got too heated, I said "Hold on. Quick time out. I got something for you." I reached into my briefcase again, pulled out a gift-wrapped package and handed it to him. What do you do when someone hands you a wrapped gift? You stop and unwrap it, right? What a perfect pattern interrupt, where a radical shift in tone and subject provides an opportunity to return to the previous subject with a fresh start, erasing your opponent's previous position.

He opened the package and inside was a book. It was called *How to Avoid Love and Marriage*. He burst out laughing. I then told him to go to some specific pages. He laughed even harder. It was three different sections that all related to stories he had shared with me about the frustrations he was having with his new fiancée. Nothing bad, just those funny things like realizing you grabbed the wrong-colored socks to go with your suit when you have a big meeting the next day and are staying at her place. That you drove home and realize you grabbed her housekeys instead of your own and need to turn around and drive back. He was in stitches.

Then I said "Jim, who knows you so well that we can push back and forth to get the school the best product, delivering exactly what you want and also laugh our butts off all in the same meeting?"

Still laughing, he nodded in agreement.

"So let's just keep growing everything together." I stuck out my hand and he shook it.

He told his assistant Bill, "Go across the hall to your office and just renew everything for another 3 years."

When we went back into his office Bill said, "Jim actually had no intention of renewing with you. What the heck happened in there? It was like watching two high powered divorce attorneys go at it and the next thing I see is you guys laughing, being buddies and we are just renewing everything exactly as it was."

I forget what I told him.

The reality was I *knew my opponent*. You see, three years earlier when I first met Jim, his then-assistant stopped him in the hallway and asked him for some advice before he went into a meeting. He asked for negotiation advice. He told Jim he was negotiating a contract with a vendor and the vendor was being really tough and a total pain to come to terms with. I remember it like it was yesterday. Jim said, "I love negotiating with that guy. A real man's man. He will get in your face and really push the limits. I like negotiating with him. He has balls and I respect that. Deal with it. It is just his style."

I filed that information away. Wow, what a gift.

You see there are many different negotiation styles. **Preparation**, including **knowledge about your opponent's style and game plan** can be very valuable. In major negotiations, it is essential.

> **PRO TIP:** I'm not advocating you should always get in your opponent's face and be theatrical as part of your negotiating strategy. I am suggesting you develop a varied negotiating toolbox. The right tool for the right situation is worth thousands. By the way: that $9.95 book made me $100K.

Your Negotiation Beliefs

Let's take a little pop quiz. Your beliefs, assumptions and a variety of myths will greatly impact your negotiation effectiveness. Take the following True/False quiz. The answers will help you understand your negotiation best practices and uncover areas that can hinder effectiveness.

Test Your Negotiation Skills in 2 Minutes

(Answer True or False)

1. Two thirds of your negotiation success is based on pre-negotiation planning
2. Most opponents use the same tactics in each of their negotiations
3. The best way to win a negotiation is to satisfy your opponent's needs
4. Negotiation is a structured process, often predictable, and can be analyzed
5. The most effective negotiation process is to be hard-nosed and confrontational
6. The best way to control a negotiation is with questions
7. Non-verbal communication tells you more than words
8. Each side's beliefs set the tone for the negotiation and how it unfolds
9. A successful negotiation strategy is wasting time on needless points
10. Most people negotiate daily.

Let's look at each of the answers to gain a quick understanding of how to create a successful negotiation strategy where everyone comes out a winner:

1. True. Very few people approach a negotiation with adequate planning. The more time spent planning, the greater the odds of a successful outcome. Typically, a team spends less than half the time required to adequately prepare for a negotiation. The primary reason for this is because they spend the majority of the time thinking through their strategy and points

of view while spending minimal time on that of their opponent. Your opponent is the other side. Spend adequate time seeing things from their viewpoint. Few people do this.
2. True. People keep going back to what has worked for them in the past. In a negotiation, past behavior is a great predictor of future behavior, strategies, and approaches. Review what your opponent has done in the past, whether with you or in negotiations with others. They will likely take the same playbook into the negotiation with you. Remember to mix it up a bit on your end. Avoid being overly predictable. Stay creative and find new ways to be more effective.
3. True. If you can satisfy the needs of your opponent while protecting or achieving your desired outcomes the negotiation will be a win for all sides.
4. True. By creating a formal planning process, outlining your objectives, and developing a 360-degree view you can anticipate much of the negotiation. Awareness of each step will allow you to review what worked and what didn't.
5. False. At times being hard-nosed is required. However, that approach right out of the gate sets the tone for a battle. Once your opponent digs in you actually lose leverage and slowed momentum toward a deal that works for everyone.
6. True. Ask the right questions and you gain a tremendous amount of power. The right questions allow you to uncover what is most important to your opponent. This allows you to guide the negotiation toward that of a Win–Win. A win–lose negotiation often yields less favorable results for all parties.

7. True. More than half of what we feel or think is communicated via body language. Be aware of your opponent's body language. It will be a more accurate gauge of how things are progressing than their words.
8. True. If you anticipate a fight you will likely have a fight. Establish an environment where both sides work to get a deal done. A deal that serves both sides interests.
9. True. Time is a valuable commodity. If one side is under a time pressure to get the deal done then the side that is being a "time waster" might be able to gain leverage. The side feeling the pressure of time my give additional concessions just to speed things up.
10. True. Most people have the opportunity to negotiate something daily. They do not notice this and that creates weak negotiation muscles. Use the opportunity to negotiate daily to heighten your awareness. When you often practice negotiating on the small things you will be more effective when it really matters.

One tactic to MASTER Negotiations

There are numerous approaches to negotiations and lots of nuances. Most people think that they need to learn the gambits and maneuvers that counter the strategies the other party might throw at them. Although that can be helpful, it is really a fairly small aspect of what will make you a successful negotiator.

As a business owner rather than an operator, you are continually taking on the role of leader. We are not going to overcomplicate the negotiation process. As a *7-figure* business owner, you understand that the simplicity and effectiveness of your processes is one of the things that allows you to scale and duplicate your successes.

In a negotiation, there is one core principle that changes everything: THINK MORE ABOUT YOUR OPPONENT'S VIEWPOINT THAN YOUR OWN.

This principle is so important. I specifically trained contract and purchasing teams at various aircraft and energy firms on how to use it. The principle became their Rosetta Stone to continually get more of what they wanted in each negotiation.

If you plan like your opponent, if you walk in your opponent's shoes, then you can start to *think like your opponent*. You become a mind reader, in a sense. And if you know what they are thinking, anticipate their motivations, their desires, their fears, their pain points and more, you can develop a highly effective strategy.

Planning your negotiation as if you were the on the other side of the table is your secret weapon.

> **PRO TIP:** 65% of your negotiation prep should be spent working through all aspects of thinking like your opponent. Work through multiple scenarios as if you were sitting in their boardroom working with them to help plan their negotiation with you. You must dedicate a significant amount of time to this step.

You already know *your* firm's main desires and motivations. You already know *your* tactics, your approaches. You do not need to rehash this over and over again. Most of that info is already known.

What you don't know is what *your opponent* is thinking. That is why this is the area where a significant amount of time needs to be spent. Invest the time in figuring out their assumptions and in planning for the multitude of ways they could be thinking. Success comes from improving on what you don't know and focusing on where you are weak. Put the time into thinking like your opponent NOT yourself.

Using The Dream Deal Scale

Let's first start with the desired deal. Understand there is more than one outcome:

- There is the **DREAM** deal — everything you desire, a home run — Let's call that an A+
- There is the **REALISTIC** deal — it's good for you, with some give and take — a solid B+
- There is your **FLOOR** — you can live with it, but anything less would be bad — your C+
- Then there is time to **WALK** — you need to know this in advance — These deals are D/F

You must map out each *in advance*. Put each in writing before walking into your negotiation. You must know how you *define each of them*. Clarity on this is *POWER*.

If you know your dream deal in advance you will be much more resistant to dropping to terms that are at a "B" or "C" level rather than an "A."

If you and your management team know your "A" and "B" level outcomes, your team is going to work hard to get them. Your team is not going to come into your office bragging about the great deal they got done when it is barely at a "C" level of desired outcome.

Sometimes the "C" level deal might be the best you can get. The point is the team needs to know what type of deal they delivered. You need to know what kind of deal you got.

The Secret to Tipping the Dream Deal Scale in Your Favor

Although it is important to map out each of your deal levels there is an even more important set of deal levels you need to map out and prep for. That's right, you need to think through, anticipate and prepare for the different scenarios (deal levels) that your opponent has. How is the other side defining their A, B, C, and D level outcomes?

As you map everything out from your opponent's vantage point you will likely notice their deal ranking chart is inverse to yours. Their *dream* is your *floor* or lower. Their *floor* is likely similar to your dream level. Somewhere in between is likely the sweet spot for everyone, a "Realistic Deal" for all parties.

As you gain a greater understanding of your opponent's *dream deal* and anticipate each of the other deal levels from their viewpoint, you move closer to becoming a master negotiator.

> **PRO TIP:** The master negotiator actually works to help the opponent *get as much of their dream deal as possible without hurting their own position*. As the master negotiator, you know that if the opponent is getting what *they* need then they are satisfied and therefore can give *you* what you need, too.

Often both parties can get everything they need. Some people are so busy fighting on small points they fail to structure the deal in a way that really works for everyone.

Keep Your Eye on The Prize

One of my clients quickly grew their sewer repair business from zero to multiple seven figures in only a few years. They decided to sell in order to pursue some new ventures. They were fully ready for life's next opportunity and truly ready to exit. They quickly received an offer that was just shy of $2,000,000. A month before the sale there were some contract points that needed to be smoothed out before closing the deal.

The Dream Deal Formula allowed them to stay focused on the prize of exiting.

The first point we were negotiating was a warranty on work they had done on prior sewer jobs. The new owner did not want to be financially on the hook for work the company had done previously. My client, the current owner, didn't want the liability and was fearful of getting hit with a large bill if an old sewer repair project needed to be covered by them.

By focusing our negotiation plan from the buyer's perspective rather than their own, we were quickly able to get ego and fear pushed aside. Clarity on potential solutions quickly emerged.

We recognized that from the buyer's viewpoint they were buying a business that claimed superior craftsmanship always promoted a message of integrity and always stood behind the quality of their work.

The buyer was essentially another customer. He wanted those same guarantees. When we viewed it that way, i.e.

through the buyer's eyes, their request made sense and that got ego out of the way.

Then we looked at *facts* rather than *fears*. How often did a sewer line actually require an additional repair? The answer was "rarely." But rarely is too vague. We looked at the number of jobs that required additional repair in each of the last 5 years. It turned out that only two or three jobs needed any additional work and in each case it was a minor tweak. The total cost was maybe $10,000 in each of those years. As we reviewed the risks, the worst-case situation it could be was possibly $20,000 and that was highly unlikely.

I then asked my client where $2 million ranked on the *Dream Deal* Scale. They said, "At the top." As we reviewed the other levels of the scale, they recognized that even $1.5 million would be reasonable, although not perfect. Essentially the lower end of the Realistic Level on our scale.

To gain greater clarity we asked more questions amongst ourselves:

"Would you be willing to discount the sale 1% to get close to your dream exit?" Yes.

"Are you extremely confident in the workmanship?" Yes, and it had gotten even better every year.

"Is it highly unlikely any repairs close to $20,000 would be required?" Yes.

"Should the new buyer be confident too?" Yes.

"Isn't 1% of 2 million only $20,000?" Yes

"Even if $50,000 was put aside to cover emergency repairs, aren't they far above their B+ Realistic Deal Level, and still pretty close to the ideal Dream Deal Level?" YES!!!

"You wouldn't be worried if you continued to own the business and the new buyer is safe too?" Yes.

In the privacy of their own office, my client gained the clarity needed to go back to the negotiation table calmly. With ego and fear removed, they were able to structure a warranty that made the buyer feel safe, secure and confident about buying the business. They were able to work for the other side's needs while also working for their own.

There were other issues ranging from value and age of equipment, and to how to retain key personnel. In each case, issues of ego and fear were where their mind jumped to first. In each case we stopped, and reviewed the issues from the new buyer's viewpoint.

We knew the business, the equipment, and the personnel; the new buyer didn't. By working through each of the points of concern as part of the negotiation planning process, and by understanding how every level of the *Dream Deal Scale* was *impacted from both sides* we mapped out multiple solutions. Solutions that worked for everybody. In each case the solution was not necessarily perfect for either side, but extremely fair, reasonable and sensible for everyone. This resulted in mapping out a deal that was a win for everybody.

Questions are your best friend

A negotiation is essentially a sale and, just like in a sale, you are working to help meet somebody else's needs. The key to meeting someone's needs is to understand those needs. By using the F.U.E.L. questions we covered in Chapter 3 you can easily guide your opponent toward a deal that makes sense for everyone.

Set a good tone in the negotiation by asking questions that develop rapport. Most people want to get a deal done and it is easier with good rapport.

To get your needs met most effectively in the negotiation, you need to get the other side's needs met, too. Ask questions about their difficulties, their concerns and their problems. Learn what issues they are trying to avoid. Learn what pitfalls they are working to prevent.

When you know their issues, use your expertise to *help them get as many of their needs met as possible while simultaneously protecting your interests*. In many cases you can give people what they want while also getting everything *you* want.

"What ifs" and "but ifs" can kill deals. Don't let fear and ego kill your deals. If something is possible but highly unlikely, find solutions and work around it.

Much of your negotiation ability and its success are based on your ability to ask good questions. Good questions have the other side share what they need to accomplish. That doesn't need to be a secret. On the contrary, if you know what the other side really needs you should work to help them get it.

> **PRO TIP:** The other side doesn't always know how to express their needs in a way that does not sound adversarial. It is your job to *read between the lines* and hear what they *need* rather than what they are *saying* they want.

This point is illustrated between parents and children. A teenager says they want to go downtown to a concert on a Saturday night with their friends. The parents say "no" or "You can't be out that late." In many instances, it is not that the parents don't want the teenager to go. Instead, it is that they don't know who they are going with, or how they are going to get home, or the expense.

The parent and teenager argue. If the issue about safety was expressed instead of transportation or money it would be easier to solve. But communication, especially in a heated discussion, goes south and rapport is lost.

In this case, if one side worked for the other's needs a solution could be found. Maybe the teenager buys the tickets or agrees to use a car service or allows the parents to drive them to the show or a combination of solutions is utilized.

Work for the *other side's* needs. Hear their *real* need. Understand their *true concern*.

Do that, and deals get done faster and easier.

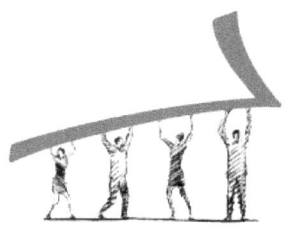

PILLAR 7
PROCESSES —
GETTING YOUR LIFE BACK

Pulling it all together: You are now an owner. Each department has specific functions and each team member has specific responsibilities, along with standards that must be met.

There are numerous steps, tasks and skills you need to consistently implement to grow your business to the level of 7 Figures and beyond.

Although not always easy, each step is very doable and each is fully within your ability. We've covered the core elements of each step. No need to overcomplicate it, the magic is in *just doing*. Each day you take another step forward on marketing, sales, customer service and managing the team with accountability is a day where you will be climbing higher and higher. Consistently take action on each step and you will enter the 7 Figure Club and, if you choose, even the Elite 8 Figure Club.

Have 7 Figures and a Life, Too

The goal is to own a business and not have the business own you. That only happens if you add in a "secret ingredient." Without it you will remain self-employed, and be the most overworked "employee" within your firm rather than being a business owner. You will have a highly compensated position — especially if you implement each of the Pillars covered in the prior chapters, but you will have a position that also comes with the high price of being anchored to the job.

The term "secret ingredient" is not an understatement. In my work with thousands of businesspeople, only a small fraction of them have utilized this key step prior to working together. Many have been on their way to growing a significant enterprise. Their income had grown to put them in the upper 1% category. But without the "secret ingredient" they each had a job with long hours rather than a business that gave them both income *and* freedom.

Trading the 40 hour a week job for a self-employed 80 hour a week job — even if high paying — is not the goal. The goal is to *cut the hours in half* — possibly choosing to work only 20 hours a week OR FEWER — all while exponentially increasing your income.

20 hours per week of work and an upper 1% income = GOOD.

80 hours per week of work regardless of the income = BAD.

And when you find all those extra hours keep you from your children and your other loved ones, disconnect you from your hobbies, prevents you from exercising and eating right, stress you out and have you paying other tolls besides those LONG HOURS, then it is REALLY BAD.

> **PRO TIP:** You must set the business up to serve you. Our goal is to be an ELITE member of the 7 Figure Club. A business OWNER who has a 7 Figure Business, an upper 1% income and the time and resources to enjoy life on their terms. *Set the business up to serve you.*

The "Work 80 Hours Per Week" Success Myth

I remember being in my 40's and moving my business into the 7 Figure Club. During that time, I set the foundation to really grow and I was fortunate enough to break that ceiling and enter the Elite 8 Figure club. The fascinating thing was that with the higher level of growth came fewer hours NOT longer hours.

The funny thing is, I could have put in far fewer hours along that journey. Graduating to business *owner over operator* was both financially rewarding and freeing. I'm so thrilled to be able to help other "business operators" become "business owners," CEOs who have the business work for them.

One of my businesses was a digital ad agency. We managed Google Pay Per Click advertising as well as SEO for well over 100 clients. When I first started the agency, I was absolutely "self-employed." I was not owning the business, I was working in it.

I remember the early days when I had only a dozen clients and started to see some money come in.

What a great feeling, especially since I was six figures in debt. Oops, I made a few bad business mistakes, trusted a few of the wrong people, and so forth, but that's a story for another day.

At the point where I had 20 clients, I saw I could realistically get 20 more thus doubling my business. I started hiring people. I expanded into larger office space. I upped my sales efforts. I started running regular meetings. And YES, increasing my hours.

I was having a great time enjoying the business growth. Validated by each new sale, I was growing a large client roster. I was in charge, with regular staff meetings, directing the troops, building accountability and orchestrating our forward momentum. The business continued to grow.

And the hours, stress, and demands of the business grew, too.

One Thanksgiving we had so much going on. I felt so important and so essential to the business. I was so close to everything. However, I couldn't see everything I was still missing.

There is a saying, "We know what we know and we don't know what we don't know."

Boy was that true. I knew so much about each aspect of the business. By managing the stats I had my fingers directly on the pulse of marketing, sales, customer service, and staff accountability. And more.

With more growth came more stress.

There was always a monkey on my back. Always something to worry about. After all, it was my business. My name was on everything. I heard and believed "The buck stops here" and I was fully aware that my identity and pride were deeply rooted in the success of the business, too.

As the business grew, so did my sense of self-worth as well as my net worth. It was what I asked for, but at the same time I was trapped.

What a dilemma.

With all the business growth, I was actually living exactly what I wrote out in my goals.

But I wasn't supposed to be putting in 80 hours a week, which I clearly recognized that Thanksgiving weekend.

Similar to many other weeks throughout the year, I had put in 40 hours by Wednesday night. I would actually say that with such pride. I viewed other people that only put in 30 hours by Wednesday as slackers. No wonder their businesses were not growing at our pace.

I believed all those hours were a necessity. Spoiler alert — That is a Myth.

It is not the time that is the must — it is that secret ingredient I kept leaving out.

So there I was on a holiday weekend. I had already put in a full week by most people's standards by that Wednesday and the family is all gathered at the house for dinner. Everyone came early so we could spend extra time catching up over drinks and appetizers prior to our Thanksgiving feast.

After about an hour I said, "Excuse me. I just need to work on a few things since we have another major deadline, please call me about 15 minutes before dinner is served."

It seemed fine, even normal, to me to do that. And as you would expect, everyone asked me all about the new projects over dinner. It all seemed so justified. Then after dinner while plates were being cleared and there was a nice gap before we put out the 7 different desserts we had, I once again excused myself just to wrap up what I had been working on. There was always just a little more work to do.

Stop the madness! Break the addiction!

Yes, there are some stages of the business where a massive amount of time and effort is required. That may be a *stage* but it is not part of the 7 Figure Club business owner's long-term lifestyle.

No matter how much you love what you do — and you *should* love it — if you really want to grow the business you need the "secret ingredient" that will allow you to structure your business as an entity bigger than you, rather than a job that requires your never-ending sacrifice.

What is the secret ingredient, the extra ingredient that almost all business owners leave out?

The Secret Ingredient?

The secret ingredient is PROCESSES.

You must have processes for everything.

Once you realize this, you have made the major leap to truly being a business owner rather than being self-employed.

You are set to be able to scale the business to 7 and 8 Figures.

You are set to experience growth and higher profits all while reducing your hours.

Spending your time in the business becomes a choice rather than a requirement.

Read that again: Spending your time in the business becomes *a choice* rather than a requirement!

Sometime that Thanksgiving night as I reflected on everything I liked about the business, I started asking why I was so involved in every department. Why was I so busy training each new person or even worse worrying about what if a particular key person was to leave? I was totally consumed with overseeing what was done right and what needed tweaking in each and every area.

One of my business mentors at the time told me "You need to review things with the team 20 times."

I would vent or complain about how I had explained to various team members how to do something. I explained it in detail. They confirmed they understood the directions but there were still 'breakdowns." So, I thought "Okay, I just need to weather the storm and endure the bumps because I only explained something 3 times or 5 times, not 20.

Well, that is a myth. You ***do not*** need to say something or explain something 20 times to your team members.

If you are doing that you have a problem. Fix it fast. Way before that 20th time.

Great Processes Set You FREE

If you have great processes, you are on your way to really building a business. Name a big business, reference a business owner that has multiple locations or a business owner that has a thriving enterprise while not being continually hands on, and I guarantee you will be looking at a business that is highly processed-based.

The franchise model is at its core a business that sells its processes, its formula, to want-to-be entrepreneurs. Think about Subway, McDonald's, The UPS Store. They each have very specific processes for everything.

Go into any of those businesses and the experience is identical. Grab a Subway sandwich in New York, California or any of their thousands of locations in between, and it will be the same. The bread looks and tastes the same, the amount of meat used is the same, the position of each veggie is the same. All duplicable.

Go to McDonald's and the menu is the same. The specials are the same, the décor is essentially the same. Each franchise has their formula, and it works.

Every business owner knows great people allow their business to run smoothly and make things easier for the owner. They also know great people are hard to find. We all want them and there are not enough to go around.

The average small business owner has a great deal of trouble staffing their business. When they finally do get a good person, they fear them leaving. And when that good or great employee does leave, it leaves a hole in the business. The small business owner often has trouble hiring 5 people. Hiring 10 becomes a chore and an interruption to the business. The undertaking of hiring 20, 30 or 50 is almost impossible to comprehend.

Finding an endless supply of great people is not a realistic expectation. It is also very much out of the business owner's control. There are countless conditions that present obstacles to hiring. Cash flow, competition, market conditions, the current labor pool and the time to train new people can become a black hole that steals any free time from the business owner.

> **PRO TIP:** Finding great or even reasonably reliable people is hard for any business owner. The solution is to create GREAT processes.

Creating great processes can solve your labor issue. Great processes are far easier to create than finding great people. They are easier to create than finding even average people. Most importantly, great processes allow average people to perform great and deliver outstanding results.

PILLAR 7: Processes

How to Create Your Processes

Creating a great process will set you free from so many business challenges. If you have a continuous business challenge in a specific area of your business look at your process or — *more likely* — *lack* of process.

Create a process for every aspect of your business. I do mean *every* aspect of the business. From how the phone is answered, to how a message is taken and delivered, to how your given widget is made. Every facet of the business turned into a process. Sales presentations — a process. Invoicing — a process. Your hiring interview and onboarding, a process. Empowering staff to solve customer service issues — a process. Each and every aspect of the business must have a process.

It is up to you as the business owner to make sure your business has solid processes.

If you have an area of the business that is weak — look at the process. Improve it.

Then, after creating a good solid process, you also need to make sure the process is followed. If you continually have reasons not to follow a process, you are undermining that process. Part of the process of managing your team is to make sure you follow the process of making sure processes are followed. *You must even have a process for making sure processes are followed.*

Friends would tease, or complain, when they would call the office because my staff always put them through the same series of questions each time they called.

When they called, the staff always answered the phone the same way.

A friend would call and say "Can I speak with Mark?"
The staff responded with "Who is calling please?"

Followed by "What company are you with and what is this regarding?"

I'd recall my friend Liviu tell me "Why do they always ask me the same questions? They should just put me through. I told them I was a friend."

I politely said "Thank you" to Liviu and the countless other friends that said the same thing, but I let them know the staff was doing exactly as they were instructed, following the call answering and screening process. In Liviu's case he was the only person I knew by that unique name but what about the Joes, Toms and Tracys that would call? In each case I had multiple friends by those names and multiple clients with those names as well.

By the staff following the protocol of the process, I knew which friend was calling and what it was about. This allowed me to decide if the call should be taken or if I should wait, thus protecting the most valuable resource, time.

If it was a client calling, the same process allowed me to know which client it was and why they were calling. Once again, I was empowered to choose to take action now or later. It also empowered me to delegate responding. In many cases a staff person could respond with what was needed. Interestingly, in many cases a staff person was actually better equipped to answer their question. If I had taken the call I would have given them a less complete answer, or possibly even needed to call them back. The process actually made things more efficient for everyone.

This all came from having a process for something as simple as answering the phone and doing proper screening.

We also had a process for how the message was taken and for making sure the message was properly passed along. These processes were the beginning of a corporate culture based on everything having a process.

The creation of those very basic processes led to every department having a comprehensive manual. Every manager developed the habit of creating detailed directions for every task within their department. For example, HR had a process for placing an ad, a process for screening applicants, an interview checklist and specific interview questions to ask based on position, testing and how to administer the tests, how to onboard people, etc. The sales department had processes for onboarding new reps, training them on presentations, establishing the benchmarks they were expected to hit, how to fill out reports and so much more. Each department's manager even had a checklist of what was required to get someone up to speed and in what timeframe.

> **PRO TIP:** A process is nothing more than written instructions on how to do a given task or function.

> **PRO TIP:** A proper process means you have formal written instructions that can be printed out and handed to someone. It can be part of a manual or file for a specific position or for the entire team.

The Process-Creation Formula

Creating processes for everything is actually pretty easy. You can literally have physical binders and electronic files for every task performed in each and every department.

All that is required to have that happen relatively quickly is to have **A PROCESS for *creating* processes.** That process is also pretty simple.

10 Simple Steps to Document Your Process

1. Have clarity on which tasks need a process and why
2. Recognize that your process is essentially a training tool.
3. When training someone, have them take detailed written notes on what they are being taught. These notes are to be typed up. If drawings, screenshots or photos are required to illustrate points, have your trainee include those as well or create them if necessary.
4. Next have the trainee do the task by carefully following the instructions they have written while you observe.
5. You observe them doing the task by following their written directions aka the first draft of a newly written process WITHOUT you giving additional instruction.
6. Anytime they are stuck due to something missing or being unclear in the instructions, the "instructor" guides the trainee and helps them perfect the instructions.
7. All edits or additions to instructions are always in writing. The instructions should now be even more detailed.
8. The trainee once again goes through the task being documented. Ideally, they can complete the task without getting stuck on any given step.
   If they are stuck due to the instructions being incomplete repeat steps 6, 7 and 8 until they get it right.
9. Test the completed version with another member of your team.
   Have them follow the instructions and observe. If the instructions are clearly and easily followed your instructions are solid. The more people that can duplicate completing the task by only following the instructions, the better the instructions are.

7. Congratulations! You have a great process and a new procedure in place. Celebrate!

The more thoroughly each area of your business is covered by written processes, the more you can scale.

Processes reduce your training time moving forward. You will be able to get new hires up to speed more quickly.

Also Use Video

Instead of waiting till you have a new person to train, you can record a Zoom call of you going through each step of a particular task or use a video messenger tool such as Loom to create an instantly shareable video. Go through each step and clearly explain what you are doing along the way. Remember to call out each step as you go. If you just talk through each element as you go, it is easy for a newbie to miss one of the steps you covered.

By "call out each step" I mean you must actually say "Step 1," "Step 2," and so on before each step: "Step 1 is ____ What you do in step one is ____, ____, and ____. For step 2 you do the following." If you outline each step really clearly, the person watching can even turn the video into written instructions if you haven't done that already.

You're No Longer a Hostage

Many entrepreneurs tolerate unsatisfactory employee behavior or performance because they need that employee to do a given task or set of tasks. The business owner doesn't want to get pulled back into doing the task, they may not even know how to do the task or they don't have anyone else that can do it, so they tolerate an employee they know is delivering a subpar contribution to the organization.

They are frozen, afraid to let an employee go or afraid to confront an employee because they would be stuck without that person. The equation is not supposed to work that way. To scale the business each role and job function needs to be supported by a set of processes not individuals.

This is very important: The good people in your organization should be honored. Appreciate each of them. Appreciate that a significant portion of their day, not to mention a significant portion of their life, is spent making your firm and your life better. Always honor that.

Having strong, solid processes does not diminish the value of any employee. It actually helps them and helps you support them. The processes allow you to promote people much more quickly. You can more easily move a wider variety of people into new roles. This also allows you to take someone out of a given role and promote them into a new and more challenging role. Formal WRITTEN processes are essential to everyone's upward mobility.

If you have the right processes, you can't be held hostage by an employee.

Even worse than being held hostage by the fear of an employee being indispensable to a particular task is the business owner holding themselves hostage.

Many business owners stifle their own growth because no one else can do a given task but them. That is ridiculous. Business *owners* build processes and in turn build up their people. Business *operators* get stuck in the self-importance of no one being able to do a task but them.

UPS, McDonald's, Subway each have 1000s of employees. They have hundreds of positions each supported by specific written procedures. The procedures are what allows them to train quickly and get consistent, predictable results from a diverse group of people.

> **PRO TIP:** Your processes are your playbook, your recipe book, your key to owning a business rather than being stuck in the role of business operator.

Why Create Processes

They save time! They make your life easier! They help you get your life back!

You want your time to be spent working *on* the business, not *in* the business. Your business can only give you the life you desire when you graduate from business operator to business owner. You can only do this if you have effective processes.

It is worth every minute spent developing each and every process. When you are busy developing your business, so many of the days can feel overwhelming. Everyday seems to have a longer to-do list than the time available permits.

Processes SAVE TIME. That feeling of being overwhelmed, that lack of time, is precisely why you must have processes developed.

One of the biggest time-wasters is doing a task more times than necessary. One of the biggest reasons we need to repeat tasks is because of mistakes. Someone left something out, forgot to check a box, did not proof all aspects of a project or just did it incorrectly or inefficiently. How many times in your organization have you seen the same mistake repeated over and over again? How many times have you told someone how to do something? Each time you repeat yourself, time is lost. When someone keeps making mistakes it is demoralizing for all involved. It erodes confidence.

Time is money and mistakes cost us time. A good process eliminates mistakes. The time you spend creating a good process is FAR BRIEFER than all the time you, your managers and your staff spend on the "do overs" required to fix a mistake.

Many of those mistakes can be eliminated with a process that can be as simple as a checklist.

Save yourself some time and get cranking on establishing those processes.

Do so with a business owner mindset. That means you either delegate process creation or you take it on with a smile knowing you are choosing to work on your business rather than be stuck in the operations of your business.

Why did it take so long?

How often have you wondered why a task took a member of the team so long to complete? Whether you have a business making cupcakes, washing cars, processing insurance claims, making 60-second real estate videos or cleaning pools, there is a standard amount of time it takes to do that thing.

The amount of time required for a given a task can be specified in the process. That way the expectation is clearly defined. This increases accountability right from the start thus improving production.

Someone who knows how to do something well typically does it more quickly. Their speed is not only based on being familiar with the task and the expertise they developed over time. It is also based on the fact that people that are good at something have found ways to be more efficient. Their efficiency, their time hacks, are all part of their process. All of which can be included in your documented processes.

This makes it possible for anyone who takes on the task to achieve the predicted performance.

Even those that already know how to do something well can improve. You may have someone in a role who is very good at their assigned tasks. They may be gifted or have a natural aptitude for it. That does not guarantee they know the most efficient way to get the task done.

I was on a trek with someone who was an experienced hiker. He was well prepared with a fully stocked backpack. We were climbing higher that day and were going to be experiencing several temperature changes. We were also planning a lunch break midway through. He had a fleece plus an additional layer. Also among his gear was a headlamp and lunch.

We were trekking along and he stopped to put on a layer. Out came the heavy jacket, the headlamp and a number of other items. He finally got the fleece, put it on and away we went. Ninety minutes later we stopped for lunch. Out came the heavy jacket, some various gear and finally the lunch which was at the very bottom of the pack. It was the first thing he put in the bag. He pulled it right out of the fridge that morning because he wanted to be sure not to forget it. In his mind, he was being very efficient.

Inside I was laughing hard but after a while it was frustrating rather than funny. Each stop was taking longer than required as he unpacked, searched and then repacked.

Finally, I couldn't take it any longer. Although he was a more experienced hiker, I pointed out that I was ready to go way faster each and every time. Why is that I asked? I received some type of wisecrack snarky comment in return.

It is obvious to an outsider: I had a well-thought-out process for packing my gear. The last item I would need was the heavy jacket so it was the first item I put in the bag. The headlamp was on top of that because it would be darker when the heavy jacket was needed. Lunch was midway on the hike so it was in the middle of the pack. The first thing I would need was my fleece so it was the last thing put in the bag. That meant it was on top, ready for immediate access. When the fleece was out of the bag, I was able to grab my lunch without digging through the rest of my gear. My process made me more efficient.

Many times even experienced members of the team do things less efficiently. They may have the skills but that does not guarantee they know the most efficient way to utilize those skills.

Your PROCESSES make people more efficient.

That saves time.

Which makes you money.

Good processes make your good people better and elevate your best people to a new higher standard. Again, make the time to create processes that make your team and organization better.

Teamwork Over Dependency

When you have a good process, a greater variety of people can jump in and more easily support other departments or roles.

If someone is sick and a report needs to be accessed, someone else can cover for the sick person by just viewing and following the process.

For instance, someone is out on vacation. How does another team member pick up the slack? They go to the playbook and follow the clearly written process.

A particular department gets slammed and you need all hands on deck. How does everyone get up to speed? You guessed it: They follow the process.

Expanding? Owner wants to go on a vacation? Owner wants to get something off their plate in order to take on more lucrative and stimulating projects to grow the business? Then all they need to do is delegate with confidence. Where does that confidence come from? Quality processes. Processes are your key to building an efficient and effective team. Your 7 Figure Club business continues to grow as you become more and more reliant on processes and less reliant on any particular person in a particular role. Processes are the foundation of your business's scalability and *your freedom to get your life back as an owner*.

> **PRO TIP:** You must become process driven.

What processes do you need?

The earlier you gain clarity on needing and utilizing processes to drive each department, the quicker you will get out of the self-employed business operator's club and in to the business owner's club.

The first step is to prioritize which processes you need.

If you have no employees then:
1. List all the roles you have in the business. Essentially everything.
8. Under each role, list all the tasks you perform in that role
9. Next to each task write down how much time you spend on that task
10. Total how much time you spend in that role daily, weekly, monthly

11. Write down how much people are paid to do that task in other organizations (calculate hourly).

What will jump out is where you are spending your time, and how much your time is really worth when doing that task. I was running a mastermind group and we were discussing how time was a big challenge. Each of us grumbled about how we were pulled in numerous directions and that many tasks pulled us away from what we really wanted to be doing.

One of the members, Larry Weiss, Founder and President of *"Atlantic Tomorrow's Office,"* spoke up. (He had over 200 employees at that time and has now grown to over 350 employees.) He shared words of wisdom that immediately stuck with me. When you are doing the task of a $15/hour staff member, you are only worth $15/hour.

Wow, that landed powerfully. Each member of the mastermind group let that settle in. We each thought of ourselves as highly paid business people. We each were highly profitable. But when we were doing the work of a lower-paid staff member, in that moment their wage was all we could value our own productivity and time. Powerful.

When doing the work of an admin your hourly value is that of an admin. When doing the work of a lead-generator your hourly value is the same as theirs. When doing the work of the line crew you are essentially another member of the line crew.

Calculate Your Hourly Value

When you see how much you are worth in specific roles or while doing specific tasks, you will immediately be motivated to spend more time in the areas that make you more money. Anything less is costing you money.

Review your list of roles and tasks along with the hourly value of each one. Select the lowest-paying items where the largest amounts of time are spent. Get yourself out of those roles and spend your time where you are most valuable.

> **PRO TIP:** Sometimes the most valuable role is not work-related. In the early stages of your business, you typically trade time for money. As you become highly profitable you may choose to trade money for time.

Jenn Drummond, the business woman and mountain climber mentioned in Pillar 1, is a great example of a true business owner that got her life back. She was very clear that spending time with each of her children was a major priority so she made it happen. She hired herself out of a job by highly compensating others to do many of the executive tasks she had been doing. This gave her the time she valued and defined as most precious.

Would you want to work for you?

It is such a powerful question to ask. My friend Michael Sonbert, founder of the firm Rebel Culture, asks that question all the time. It is a question that can transform you as a leader and thus enables you to prepare your organization for the 7 Figure Club journey. As you grow your business into a large and profitable member of the 7 Figure Club, remember to build an organization that you would want to be a part of.

"If I weren't the owner, would my organization be one I would be a part of?" It's an important question to ask yourself and your answer is equally important. If you said anything other than a confident "Yes," you need to evaluate why.

Eliminate the reasons that would deter you from wanting to be a part of your business. As you grow, more and more of your business is based on people. They are the ones that make your processes operate properly. You want them to want to be there.

If you have reasons that would keep you from wanting to work in your own business, then the people in your business are also going to feel that way. Those reasons are going to point to weaknesses in the processes at the very foundation of your business. Correct them early.

Everything is your fault

Billy Gene, founder of *"Billy Gene Is Marketing"* and host of the podcast *"Billy Gene is Marketing Offends The Internet,"* grew his business to eight figures by having a culture of excellence. Number one of his top-10 corporate-culture values is "It's all your fault." As the owner of your business it is your responsibility to own *all* aspects of the business, good and bad.

You are the one responsible for putting all the steps of the 7 Figure Club Formula in place. You are the owner taking the business higher.

I love how so many business owners take credit for the big sale, the negotiation outcome and other big wins. It is their business and the great outcomes are a result of their choices. I'm not saying they take all the credit, that's rarely the case, but they are proud of their role in the success.

I laugh when they don't take the same level of responsibility when things go wrong. Recognize it is all your fault. When there is a customer service issue, it's your fault. A sales breakdown, your fault. A bad hire, your fault. Etcetera. That's a lot of pressure. That's a lot of responsibility. And that all goes with being a leader of a thriving 7 Figure business.

It is up to you to make sure the right processes are in place, that capable people are executing those processes, that those people have a positive attitude, work ethic and appropriate values. You are ultimately responsible for each driver stat moving in the right direction. You are responsible for making sure the team delivers on the end-game results required to win at the level you defined. The outcome of everything rests on your shoulders.

Recognizing this and being honest about it is essential to have marketing, sales, and service all work in unison. It is your 7 Figure Business and you are responsible for all the elements. Yes, when it works it is due to you. The reverse is true as well.

Expect challenges. Expect bumps and bruises. Expect some days to be tough. It is all part of the game of business. Maintaining the mindset that "it ULTIMATELY is ALL on you" is essential to keep climbing higher.

It's Time to Join The 7-Figure Club

The formula is simple — don't overcomplicate it:
1. Map out your vision with clearly-written goals
2. Eliminate the guesswork of how each department is doing and how the overall health of the business is doing. Build a stats dashboard and let the facts guide you.
3. Have a solid sales process where progress is consistently measured by tracking the driver actions along with their associated results. Hold the team accountable to posting the numbers and to improving their performance.

4. Create a marketing mix based on multiple pillars that generates a high volume of quality leads. Formally measure and track both your return on ad spend (ROAS) and your return on investment (ROI). Leverage what works and eliminate the rest.
5. Build a culture where everyone is focused on delivering A.N.A.W.A.R.D.™ Winning Level of Service. Define your commitment to great service in a tangible and measurable way which is tracked.
6. Grow far beyond your comfort zone by improving business skills such as negotiation, finance, and other key areas. Continually improve, evolve, and lead by example.
7. Be a business owner rather than a business operator. Set yourself free from the day-to-day operations and create a foundation on which to scale by building a process-based business.

Follow the formula.

Implement each step.

Adjust based on your instrument readings and take the actions required to build strong numbers.

That will put you on the fast track to owning a business with sales that are in the top 10% of all small businesses and generating a top 1% income for you.

You will find yourself well positioned to Join The 7-Figure Club.

You are the **CREATOR** of your 7 Figure Business!!! Always remember that. When you *own* that revelation, you are in control of the journey.

Become a member:
JoinThe7FigureClub.com

FREE 7 FIGURE CLUB RESOURCES

The New Year Quick Start Program

This free event will have you map out your goals and share the top strategies to achieve them consistently.

Get the quick start planning guide and access to the program at **JoinThe7FigureClub.com**

The 7 Figure Sales Masterclass

This masterclass is a free training. Join Mark Anthony on a recorded training where he shares how to create a powerful sales presentation. Take your sales skills to the next level. Mark shares many of his most effective techniques taught to sales teams worldwide.

To watch the Sales Masterclass now or to sign up for a time that works best for you, visit **JoinThe7FigureClub.com**.

Other Free Bonuses

- Become part of a community of business owners climbing higher.
- Get access to bonus worksheets.
- Participate in complimentary LIVE Q & A sessions.
- Fuel your business growth.

Learn about our 7 Figure Club
Mastermind, coaching and other trainings

JoinThe7FigureClub.com

www.ingramcontent.com/pod-product-compliance
Lightning Source LLC
LaVergne TN
LVHW051827080426
835512LV00018B/2766